Gregg Shorthand

Shorthand written
by Charles Rader

GREGG

Shorthand

John Robert Gregg

Louis A. Leslie / Charles E. Zoubek

McGraw-Hill
Book Company

New York   St. Louis   San Francisco   Auckland   Bogotá
Guatemala   Hamburg   Johannesburg   Lisbon   London   Madrid
Mexico   Montreal   New Delhi   Panama   Paris   San Juan
São Paulo   Singapore   Sydney   Tokyo   Toronto

Library of Congress Cataloging in Publication Data

Gregg, John Robert, date.
  Gregg shorthand, series 90.

  Includes indexes.
  1. Shorthand—Gregg. I. Leslie, Louis A., date.
joint author. II. Zoubek, Charles E., date. joint
author. III. Title.
Z56.G813 1978   653'.427   77-4161
ISBN 0-07-024471-5 (Gregg Ed'n.)
ISBN 0-07-024490-1 (Trade Ed'n.)

  2 3 4 5 6 7 8 9 D O C D O C 8 7 6
ISBN 0-07-024490-1
First McGraw-Hill Trade Edition, 1985

Preface

Gregg Shorthand, the universal system

Gregg Shorthand was first published in 1888 and has been learned and used successfully by millions of writers throughout the entire world. Gregg Shorthand was written in English but has been successfully adapted to numerous other languages, including French, Spanish, and Portuguese. To most people the terms *shorthand* and *Gregg* are synonymous. Gregg Shorthand is truly the universal system of shorthand. It is used by more shorthand writers than any other system in the world.

Gregg Shorthand is used by stenographers and administrative secretaries as a vocational tool that enables them to obtain and hold interesting and rewarding positions. It is used by business and professional people who are relieved of the burden of writing longhand in making notes, preparing important papers, and drafting reports.

The success of any system of shorthand rests on the merits of its alphabet. The Gregg alphabet is the most logical, consistent, and efficient shorthand alphabet devised in more than 2,000 years of shorthand history. The fact that this alphabet, virtually without change, has been the basis of Gregg Shorthand for more than 90 years is a tribute to the genius of its inventor, John Robert Gregg.

Series 90

Objectives *Gregg Shorthand, Series 90,* is published in the ninetieth anniversary year of the invention of the Gregg system. This revision involves a small number of system changes which have been deemed desirable to make learning and writing Gregg Shorthand even easier and more consistent. A major change has been made in the order of presentation of the theory principles. This change was made to provide better, more logical business letters even in the very early lessons in the text. Teachers will find the system changes to be logical and the teaching and learning suggestions helpful. The major objectives of *Gregg Shorthand, Series 90,* are:

1 To teach the students to read and write Gregg Shorthand rapidly and accurately in the shortest time possible.

2 To provide the students with transcription readiness by building their vocabulary and developing their ability to spell and punctuate accurately.

Organization

Gregg Shorthand, Series 90, is divided into three parts—Principles, Reinforcement, and Shorthand and Transcription Skill Building. These parts are subdivided into 10 chapters and 70 lessons. The last new theory is presented in Lesson 47. The theory is presented in 40 lessons. Eight of the first 48 lessons are devoted to review.

Format

Gregg Shorthand, Series 90, is published in the same two-column format which proved popular in the last edition of Gregg Shorthand. This format makes it possible to present the shorthand practice material in columns that are approximately the width of the columns of the students' shorthand notebooks. The short lines make reading easier because the eye does not have to travel very far from the end of one line of shorthand to the beginning of the next. The format also makes it possible to highlight the words from the Reading and Writing Practice that are identified for spelling attention. The words are placed in the margins near the corresponding shorthand outline.

Building transcription skills

Gregg Shorthand, Series 90, continues to place great stress on the nonshorthand elements of transcription, which are taught concurrently with shorthand. It retains all the helpful transcription exercises of the former edition. These include:

Business Vocabulary Builders Beginning with Lesson 7, each lesson contains a Business Vocabulary Builder consisting of several business words or expressions for which meanings are provided. The words and expressions are selected from the Reading and Writing Practice. The Business Vocabulary Builders help to overcome a major student handicap—a limited vocabulary.

Spelling—Marginal Reminders Words singled out from the Reading and Writing Practice for special spelling attention appear in the margins of the shorthand. Usually each word appears on the same line as its shorthand outline. These words appear in a second color in the shorthand so that they are easy to see.

In *Gregg Shorthand, Series 90*, spelling is introduced in Chapter 4.

Spelling—Families An effective device for improving spelling is the study of words in related groups, or spelling families. In the Series 90 edition, the students study six spelling families, beginning with Lesson 45.

Similar-Words Drills These drills teach the students the difference in meaning between similar words that stenographers often confuse—*it's, its; addition, edition; there, their, they're*, etc.

Punctuation Beginning with Lesson 31, nine frequent usages of the comma are introduced. Only one comma usage is introduced in any given lesson. The commas are encircled and appear in the shorthand; the reason for the use of the comma is shown above the circle.

Common Prefixes An understanding of the meaning of common English prefixes is an effective device for developing the students' understanding of words. In *Gregg Shorthand, Series 90,* the students study five common English prefixes, beginning in Lesson 56.

Grammar Checkup In a number of lessons, drills are provided on rules of grammar that students often apply incorrectly.

Transcription Quiz Beginning with Lesson 57, each lesson contains a Transcription Quiz consisting of a letter in which the students have to supply internal punctuation. This quiz provides them with a daily test of how well they have mastered the punctuation rules presented in earlier lessons.

Reading and writing practice

In *Gregg Shorthand, Series 90,* there are 40,616 words of shorthand practice material in the Reading and Writing Practice exercises. Most of the material is new.

A brief-form letter is included in *every* lesson of Part 1 (except the review lessons), beginning with Lesson 5.

Other features

Shorthand spelling helps When a new letter in the shorthand alphabet or a theory principle is presented, the shorthand spelling is given.

Chapter openings Each chapter is introduced by a well-illustrated spread that not only paints for the students a picture of the life and duties of a secretary but also encourages them in their efforts to acquire the necessary skills.

Student helps To be sure that the students get the greatest benefit from each phase of their shorthand study, they are given step-by-step suggestions on how to handle each phase when it is first introduced.

Reading scoreboards At various points in the text, students are given an opportunity to determine their reading speed by means of a scoreboard. The scoreboard enables the students to calculate the number of words a minute they are reading. By comparing their reading speed from scoreboard to scoreboard, they see some indication of their shorthand reading growth.

Recall charts In the last lesson of each chapter in Part 1 a recall chart is provided. This chart contains illustrations of theory principles taught in the chapter. It also contains many illustrations of theory principles the students have studied up to that chapter.

Checklists To keep the students constantly reminded of the importance of good practice procedures, occasional checklists are provided. These checklists deal with writing shorthand, reading shorthand, homework, proportion, etc.

Appendix The Appendix contains a number of additional teaching aids. These include:

1 A brief-form chart giving all brief forms in Gregg Shorthand, Series 90, in the order of their presentation.
2 A list of common geographical expressions.
3 A chart showing Gregg outlines for common metric expressions.

Computer control

All of the connected matter in *Gregg Shorthand, Series 90*, has been checked by a carefully written computer program to ensure adequate, proper, and sequential coverage of the theory principles and brief forms. The computer program helped the authors of the book to ensure that the points were properly covered in the lessons in which they were presented as well as in the two lessons following their initial presentation.

● ● ●

Gregg Shorthand, Series 90, is published with pride and with the confidence that it will help teachers of Gregg Shorthand do an even more effective job of training rapid and accurate shorthand writers and transcribers.

The Publishers

Contents

Your Shorthand Practice Program

The speed with which you learn to read and write Gregg Shorthand will depend largely on two factors—the *time* you devote to practice and the *way* in which you practice. If you practice efficiently, you will be able to complete each lesson in the shortest possible time and derive the greatest possible benefit.

Here are some suggestions which will help you to get the maximum benefit from the time you invest in shorthand practice.

Before you begin, select a quiet place in which to practice. Do not try to practice while listening to music or watching television. Then follow the steps below.

Reading word lists

In each lesson there are a number of word lists that illustrate the principles introduced in the lesson. As part of your out-of-class practice, read these word lists in this way:

1 *With the type key available,* spell—aloud if possible—the shorthand characters in each outline in the list, thus: *"see, s-e; fee, f-e."* Reading aloud will help to impress the shorthand outlines firmly on your mind. Read all the shorthand words in the list in this way—with the type key exposed—until you feel you can read the shorthand outlines without referring to the key.

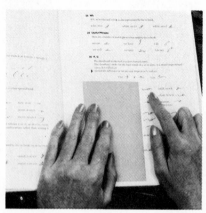

Study the word lists by placing a slip of paper over the type key and reading the shorthand words aloud.

2 *Cover the type key* with a piece of paper and read aloud from the shorthand, thus: *"s-e, see; f-e, fee."*

3 If the spelling of a shorthand outline does not immediately give you the meaning, refer to the key and determine the meaning of any outline you cannot read. Do *not* spend more than a few seconds trying to decipher an outline.

4 After you have read all the words in the list, read them again if time permits.

Note: In reading brief forms for common words and phrases, which first occur in Lesson 3, do not spell the shorthand outlines.

Reading sentences, letters, and articles

Each lesson contains a Reading Practice (Lessons 1-6) or a Reading and Writing Practice (Lessons 7-70) in which sentences, letters, or articles are written in shorthand. Proper practice on this material will help you develop your shorthand ability. First, *read* the material. Two procedures are suggested for reading shorthand—one with a *Student's Transcript* and one without a *Student's Transcript*.

Procedure With Student's Transcript If you have a *Student's Transcript* to the shorthand in this textbook, you should follow this procedure:

1 Place the *Student's Transcript* to the right of your textbook and open it to the key to the Reading Practice or the Reading and Writing Practice you are about to read.

2 Place your left index finger under the shorthand outline in the text that you are about to read and your right index finger under the corresponding word in the *Student's Transcript*.

3 Read the shorthand outlines aloud until you come to a word you cannot read. Spell the shorthand strokes in that outline. If this spelling does not *immediately* give you the meaning, anchor your left index finger on the outline and look at the transcript, where your right index finger is resting near the point at which you are reading.

4 Determine the meaning of the outline you cannot read and place your right index finger on it.

5 Return to the shorthand from which you are reading—your left index finger has kept your place for you—and continue reading in this manner until you have completed the material.

6 If time permits, read the material a second time.

By following this procedure, you will lose no time finding your place in the shorthand and in the transcript when you cannot read an outline.

Procedure Without Student's Transcript If you do not have a *Student's Transcript*, you should follow this procedure:

1 Before you start reading the shorthand, have a blank piece of paper or a blank card handy.

2 Read the shorthand aloud.

3 When you come to a shorthand outline that you cannot read, spell the shorthand strokes in the outline. If the spelling gives you the meaning, continue reading. If it does not, write the outline on your sheet of paper or card and continue reading. Do not spend more than a few seconds trying to decipher the outline.

4 After you have gone through the entire Reading and Writing Practice in this way, repeat this procedure if time permits. On this second reading you may be able to read some of the outlines that gave you trouble the first time. When that happens, cross those outlines off your sheet or card.

5 Finally—and very important—at the earliest opportunity ask your teacher or a classmate the meaning of the outlines that you could not read.

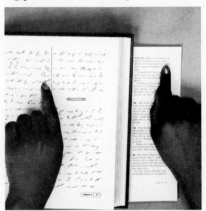

Refer to your *Transcript* whenever you cannot read an outline. Keep your left index finger anchored in the shorthand; the right index finger, on the corresponding place in the *Transcript*.

Read the Reading and Writing Practice, writing on the card any outlines that you cannot read after spelling them.

Remember, during the early stages your shorthand reading may not be very rapid. That is only natural, as you are, in a sense, learning a new language. If you practice regularly, however, you will find your reading rate increasing almost daily.

Writing the Reading and Writing Practice

Before you do any writing of shorthand, you should give careful consideration to the tools of your trade—your notebook and your writing instrument.

Your notebook The best notebook for shorthand writing is one that measures 6 x 9 inches and has a vertical rule down the center of each page. It should have a spiral binding so that the pages lie flat at all times. The paper should, of course, take ink well.

Your writing instrument A pen is a satisfactory instrument for writing Gregg Shorthand. *A pencil is not recommended.* Because writing with a pen requires little pressure, you can write for long periods of time without becoming fatigued. A pencil, however, requires considerable pressure. In addition, the pencil point quickly becomes blunt. The blunter it gets, the more effort you have to expend to write with it. Penwritten notes remain legible almost indefinitely; pencil notes become blurred and hard to read. In addition, penwritten notes are also easier to read under artificial light.

Having selected your writing tools, follow these steps in writing the Reading and Writing Practice:

1 Read the material you are going to copy. *Always* read the Reading and Writing Practice before copying it.

2 When you are ready to start writing, read a convenient group of words from the printed shorthand; then write the group, reading aloud as you write. Keep your place in the shorthand with your left index finger if you are right-handed or with your right index finger if you are left-handed.

In the early stages your writing may not be very rapid, nor will your notes be as well written as those in the book. With regular practice, however, your notes will rapidly improve.

Good luck with your study of Gregg Shorthand.

When copying, read a convenient group of words aloud and then write that group in your notebook. Keep your place in the shorthand with your left index finger.

Principles

Why Study Shorthand?

"Why should I study to perfect my shorthand skills?" "Is shorthand really necessary in today's business?" "In the world of automation, is manual shorthand skill still needed?" These are some of the questions students ask today as they prepare for careers. The answers are very clear:

Today there are more shorthand writers than ever before, and the number grows continually. Even so, the demand for secretaries in business exceeds the supply. The ability to take shorthand is a vital skill in the fast-paced world of business, a world in which recording data quickly and accurately is a necessity. So much of all business is transacted on written communications—letters, memorandums, reports, minutes—that the secretary who can take shorthand is in great demand.

Knowing shorthand is important not only when someone wants to dictate a letter or a report, but also when the phone rings and you must take a long, involved message. And what a help it is, when composing your own letters, to be able to jot down all your thoughts before they escape.

When you begin looking for your first job, you will find that the ability to take shorthand will increase your chances of getting just the position you want. The ability to use shorthand will also increase the size of your paycheck. Whether your job is as a beginning worker or is on an advanced level, in almost every case, business pays more to the secretary who can take shorthand than to the one who cannot.

The dividends continue to pay off. After you have been on a job for a while, you will discover that your shorthand ability will very likely put you in line for a promotion. Good, above-average stenographic skill combined with language ability and a desire to work will put you at the top of the list when there is a chance for a promotion.

You are now starting to learn the basics of Gregg Shorthand. Take time to learn shorthand well. Spend some out-of-class time every day studying the current lesson. You will find that your ability to read and write shorthand will grow rapidly. Follow your teacher's instructions, and you will soon have a marketable skill which you can put to work in a business office.

Shorthand is a valuable skill that can open many doors for you. The time you spend in learning shorthand is well invested.

LESSON 1

GREGG
SHORTHAND
IS EASY
TO LEARN

As you leaf through the pages of this book and see the hooks and circles and straight lines in the shorthand outlines, you may wonder whether you can learn shorthand. Be assured that you can, just as millions of others have learned it. If you can write longhand—and of course you can!—you can learn to write Gregg Shorthand. The strokes you will write in Gregg Shorthand are the same strokes that you are accustomed to writing in longhand.

Actually, you will find Gregg Shorthand easier to learn than longhand. Skeptical? Well, the following illustration should convince you of the truth of that statement. In longhand there are many ways to write *f*. Here are six of them:

$$F \quad f \quad f \quad \mathcal{F} \quad \mathcal{F} \quad \mathcal{F}$$

What is more, in many words the sound of *f* is expressed by combinations of other letters in the alphabet—for example, *ph*, as in *phase*; *gh*, as in *rough*.

In Gregg Shorthand there is one way—and only one way—to express the sound of *f*, as you will learn later in this lesson.

With Gregg Shorthand you can attain almost any speed goal you set for yourself. All it takes is regular, intelligent practice.

Principles

GROUP A

1 S-Z

The first shorthand stroke you will learn is *s*, one of the most frequently used letters in the English language. The shorthand *s* is a tiny downward curve that resembles the longhand comma.

Because in English *s* often has the sound of *z*, as in *saves*, the same tiny downward curve is used to express *z*.

S-Z

2 A

The second stroke you will learn is the shorthand *a*, which is simply the longhand *a* with the final connecting stroke omitted.

A *a* O

3 Silent Letters Omitted

In the English language many words contain letters that are not pronounced. In Gregg Shorthand these silent letters are not written.

For example, the word *say* would be written *s-a;* the *y* would not be written because it is not pronounced. The word *face* would be written *f-a-s;* the *e* would not be written because it is not pronounced, and the *c* would be represented by *s* because it is pronounced *s.*

In the following words, what letters would not be written because they are not pronounced?

right	same	day	steam
main	save	snow	aid

4 S-A Word

With the strokes for *s* and *a*, you can form the shorthand outline for a very useful word.

say, s-a ∂ ↙

5 F, V

The shorthand stroke for *f* is a downward curve the same shape as *s*, but it is somewhat larger—about half the height of the space between the lines of your shorthand notebook.

The shorthand stroke for *v* is also a downward curve the same shape as *s* and *f*, but it is very large—almost the full height of the space between the lines of your shorthand notebook.

▶ Notice the difference in the sizes of *s, f, v.*

S ﹐↙   F ﹚↙   V ﹚↙

F

safe, s-a-f 𝓎   *face, f-a-s* ∂   *safes, s-a-f-s* 𝓎

▶ Notice that the *c* in *face* is represented by the *s* because it has the *s* sound.

V

save, s-a-v *9* vase, v-a-s *𝄐* saves, s-a-v-s *9*

▶ Notice that the final *s* in *saves* has the *z* sound, which is represented by the *s* stroke.

6 E

The shorthand stroke for *e* is a tiny circle. It is simply the longhand *e* with the two connecting strokes omitted.

▶ Notice the difference in the sizes of *a* and *e*.

A *O*   E *。*

see, s-e *𝄐*   sees, s-e-s *𝄐*   ease, e-s *9*

fee, f-e *𝄐*   fees, f-e-s *𝄐*   easy, e-s-e *𝄐*

▶ Notice that the *y* in *easy* is pronounced *e;* therefore, it is represented by the *e* circle.

Suggestion   At this point take a few moments to read the procedures outlined for practicing word lists on page 10.

GROUP B

7 N, M

The shorthand stroke for *n* is a very short forward straight line.
The shorthand stroke for *m* is a longer forward straight line.

N

see, s-e *𝄐*   say, s-a *𝄐*   vain, v-a-n *𝄐*

seen, s-e-n *𝄐*   sane, s-a-n *𝄐*   knee, n-e *⟶o*

▶ Notice that the *k* in *knee* is not written because it is not pronounced.

M

me, m-e 　　main, m-a-n 　　same, s-a-m

mean, m-e-n 　　aim, a-m 　　seem, s-e-m

may, m-a 　　name, n-a-m 　　fame, f-a-m

8　T, D

The shorthand stroke for *t* is a short upward straight line.
The shorthand stroke for *d* is a longer upward straight line.

T 　　D

T

eat, e-t 　　meet, m-e-t 　　east, e-s-t

neat, n-e-t 　　seat, s-e-t 　　team, t-e-m

D

day, d-a 　　need, n-e-d 　　made, m-a-d

date, d-a-t 　　aid, a-d 　　feed, f-e-d

9　Punctuation and Capitalization

period 　\　　paragraph 　>　　parentheses 　( )

question mark 　×　　dash 　=　　hyphen 　=

The regular longhand forms are used for all other punctuation marks.
Capitalization is indicated by two upward dashes placed underneath the word to be capitalized.

Fay 　　　　Dave 　　　　May

● Reading Practice

With the help of an occasional word written in longhand, you can already read complete sentences.

Read the following sentences, spelling each shorthand outline aloud as you read it thus: *F-a, Fay; m-a-d, made; t-e, tea.* If you cannot read a shorthand outline after you have spelled it, refer to the key which follows the Reading Practice.

GROUP A

GROUP B

GROUP C

[63]

GROUP A 1. *Fay made tea for me.*   2. *I need a vase.*   3. *Meet me on East Main.*
4. *Nate made the Navy team.*   5. *Nate made a safety the same day.*   GROUP B
6. *Dave made a date for May 15.*   7. *Fay's deed is in Dave's safe.*   8. *Nate Meade may stay to aid me.*   9. *Fay's room faced East Main.*   10. *Amy saved the fee.*
GROUP C 11. *Amy may feed me.*   12. *Did Nate say, "Dave is vain"?*   13. *Nate saved $10 in May.*   14. *Amy made a date with Dean.*   15. *Dave may need aid.*

Principles

10 Alphabet Review

In Lesson 1 you studied the following nine shorthand strokes. How rapidly can you read them?

$$O \quad \circ \quad — \quad — \quad / \quad / \quad) \quad) \quad ,$$

11 O, R, L

The shorthand stroke for *o* is a small deep hook.
The shorthand stroke for *r* is a short forward curve.
The shorthand stroke for *l* is a longer forward curve about three times as long as *r*.

▶ Note how these strokes are derived from their longhand forms.

O

no, n-o	*so, s-o*	*own, o-n*
snow, s-n-o	*phone, f-o-n*	*dome, d-o-m*
tow, t-o	*note, n-o-t*	*stone, s-t-o-n*

▶ Notice that in *own, dome,* and *stone* the *o* is placed on its side. By placing *o* on its side before *n* or *m* in these and similar words, we obtain smoother joinings than we would if we wrote the *o* upright.

R

ray, r-a	*dear, d-e-r*	*more, m-o-r*
rate, r-a-t	*near, n-e-r*	*radio, r-a-d-e-o*
trade, t-r-a-d	*or, o-r*	*free, f-r-e*

L

lay, l-a

mail, m-a-l

leaves, l-e-v-s

late, l-a-t

deal, d-e-l

low, l-o

ail, a-l

feel, f-e-l

flow, f-l-o

▶ Notice that *f-r*, as in *free*, and *f-l*, as in *flow*, are written with one sweep of the pen, with no stop between the *f* and the *r* or *l*.

free   flow

12 H, -ing

The letter *h* is simply a dot placed above the vowel. With few exceptions, *h* occurs at the beginning of a word.

Ing, which almost always occurs at the end of a word, is also expressed by a dot.

H

he, h-e

hear, h-e-r

hole, h-o-l

-ing

reading,
r-e-d-ing

hearing,
h-e-r-ing

heeding,
h-e-d-ing

13 Long ī

The shorthand stroke for the long sound of *ī*, as in *high*, is a large broken circle.

I

high, h-ī

write (right),
r-ī-t

fine, f-ī-n

tire, t-ī-r

my, m-ī

side, s-ī-d

light, l-ī-t

might, m-ī-t

line, l-ī-n

14 Omission of Minor Vowels

Some words contain vowels that are slurred or not pronounced at all in ordinary speech. For example, the word *even* is really pronounced *e-vn*; the word *meter* is pronounced *met-r*. These vowels may be omitted if they do not contribute to speed or readability.

even, e-v-n

reader, r-e-d-r

later, l-a-t-r

meter, m-e-t-r *motor, m-o-t-r* *dealer, d-e-l-r*

● Reading Practice

With the aid of a few words written in longhand, you can now read the following sentences. Remember to spell each shorthand word aloud as you read it. Refer to the key when you cannot read a word.

GROUP A

GROUP B

GROUP C

[74]

GROUP A 1. Lee Stone may drive me home later. 2. My radio dealer is Dale Lee. 3. Fay's whole right side is sore. 4. Dale may remain here this evening. 5. My railroad train leaves at eight. **GROUP B** 6. Steve's train is late. 7. My reading rate is low. 8. Dave's reading rate is high. 9. Dale may fly home at Easter. 10. Steven leaves for Rome in May. **GROUP C** 11. He is feeling fine. 12. Mary dyed her hair. 13. My name is David Dearing. 14. He notified me that my tire was stolen. 15. I tore my evening dress.

Principles

15 Alphabet Review

Here are the strokes you studied in Lesson 1 and 2. How fast can you read them?

16 Brief Forms

The English language contains many words that are used over and over again. As an aid to rapid shorthand writing, special abbreviations, called *brief forms*, are provided for some of these words. For example, we write *m* for *am*, *v* for *have*.

You are already familiar with the process of abbreviation in longhand—you write *Mr.* for *Mister*, *Dr.* for *Doctor*.

Because these brief forms occur so frequently, you will be wise to learn them well!

I	◯	*are, our, hour*	⌣	*am*	—
Mr.	⌐⟩	*will, well*	⌣	*it, at*	╱
have	⟩	*a, an*	•	*in,* not*	—

*In is also used as a word beginning in such words as:

invite, in-v-ī-t ⌐ *indeed, in-d-e-d* ⟋ *inside, in-s-ī-d* ⟋

▶ Did you notice that some shorthand outlines have two or more meanings? You will have no difficulty selecting the correct meaning of a brief form when it appears in the sentence. The sense of the sentence will give you the answer.

17 Phrasing

By using brief forms for common words, we are able to save writing time. Another device that helps save writing time is called *phrasing*, or the writing of two or more shorthand outlines together. Here are a number of useful phrases built with the brief forms you have just studied.

I have	I will not	he will not
I have not	I am	are not
I will	he will	in our

18 Left S-Z

In Lesson 1 you learned one stroke for s and z. Another stroke is also used for s and z in order to provide an easy joining in any combination of strokes—a backward comma, which is also written downward. For convenience, it is called the *left* s.

At this point you need not try to decide which s stroke to use in any given word; this will become clear to you as your study of shorthand progresses.

S-Z

lease, l-e-s	needs, n-e-d-s	days, d-a-s
sales, s-a-l-s	raised, r-a-s-d	most, m-o-s-t
seems, s-e-m-s	readers, r-e-d-r-s	names, n-a-m-s

19 P, B

The shorthand stroke for p is a downward curve the same shape as the left s except that it is larger—approximately half the height of the space between the lines in your shorthand notebook.

The shorthand stroke for b is also a downward curve the same shape as the left s and p except that it is much larger—almost the full height of the space between the lines in your shorthand notebook.

▶ Notice the difference in the sizes of the left s, p, and b.

S   P   B

P

pay, p-a	opens, o-p-n-s	post, p-o-s-t
spare, s-p-a-r	pipe, p-ī-p	please, p-l-e-s
hope, h-o-p	pain, p-a-n	price, p-r-ī-s

B

bay, b-a 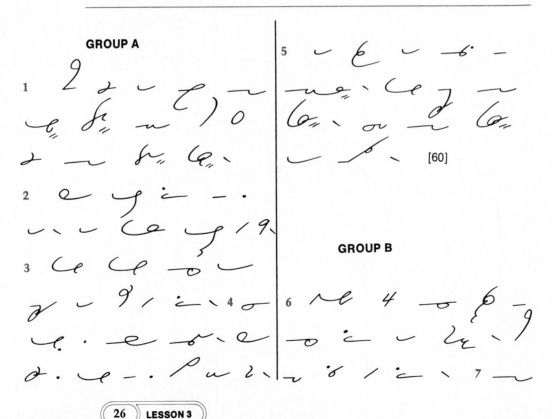   beat, b-e-t   blame, b-l-a-m

base, b-a-s   bright, b-r-ī-t   neighbor, n-a-b-r

boat, b-o-t   brief, b-r-e-f   label, l-a-b-l

▶ Notice that the combinations *p-r*, as in *price*; *p-l*, as in *please*; *b-r*, as in *brief*, and *b-l*, as in *blame*, are written with one sweep of the pen without a pause between the *p* or *b* and the *r* or *l*.

price   please   brief   blame

● Reading Practice

You can already read sentences written entirely in shorthand.

Suggestion Before you start your work on this Reading Practice, read the practice procedures for reading shorthand on page 10.

GROUP A

1

2

3

5

[60]

GROUP B

6

7

GROUP C

11 ... 12 ... 13 ...

[57]

14 ... 15 ...

[48]

GROUP D

16 ... 17 ... 18 ... 19 ... 20 ...

[54]

Principles

20 Alphabet Review

Here is a review of the 17 shorthand strokes you studied in Lessons 1 through 3. How fast can you read them?

21 OO

The shorthand stroke for the sound of *oo*, as in *to*, is a tiny upward hook.

OO ⌐

to (two, too), t-oo	room, r-oo-m	new, n-oo
do, d-oo	suit, s-oo-t	noon, n-oo-n
who, h-oo	fruit, f-r-oo-t	move, m-oo-v

▶ Notice that the *oo* is placed on its side when it follows *n* or *m*, as in *new, noon, move*. By placing the hook on its side in these combinations rather than writing it upright, we obtain smooth joinings.

22 W, Sw

At the beginning of words *w*, as in *we*, is represented by the *oo* hook; *sw*, as in *sweet*, by *s-oo*.

we, oo-e	wait, oo-a-t	sweet, s-oo-e-t
way, oo-a	waste, oo-a-s-t	swear, s-oo-a-r

23 Wh

Wh, as in *why* and *while*, is also represented by the *oo* hook.

why, oo-ī   while, oo-ī-t   white, oo-ī-t   while, oo-ī-l

24 Useful Phrases

Here are a number of useful phrases that employ the *oo* hook.

we are   we have   I do

we will   we may   I do not

25 K, G

The shorthand stroke for *k* is a short forward curve.
The shorthand stroke for the hard sound of *g*, as in *game*, is a much longer forward curve. It is called *gay*.

▶ Notice the difference in the size and shape of *oo*, *k*, and *gay*.

OO   K   Gay

K

take, t-a-k   like, l-ī-k   week, oo-e-k

make, m-a-k   keep, k-e-p   clean, k-l-e-n

cake, k-a-k   care, k-a-r   increase, in-k-r-e-s

Gay

gain, gay-a-n   great, gay-r-a-t   go, gay-o

game, gay-a-m   grade, gay-r-a-d   goal, gay-o-l

gave, gay-a-v   green, gay-r-e-n   legal, l-e-g-l

▶ Notice that *k-r*, as in *increase*, and *gay-l*, as in *legal*, are written with a smooth, wave-like motion.

increase   legal

But *k-l*, as in *clean*, and *gay-r*, as in *green*, are written with a hump between the *k* and the *l* and the *gay* and the *r*.

clean   green

● Reading Practice

The following sentences contain many illustrations of the new shorthand strokes you studied in Lesson 4. They also review the shorthand strokes, brief forms, and phrases you studied in Lessons 1 through 3.

Read these sentences aloud, spelling each shorthand outline that you cannot immediately read.

GROUP A

[shorthand outlines, sentences 1–5, ending with [43]]

GROUP B

[shorthand outlines, sentences 6–10, ending with [41]]

GROUP C

[shorthand outlines, sentences 11–14]

15 [shorthand] [48]

GROUP D

16 [shorthand] 17 [shorthand] 18 [shorthand] 19 [shorthand] 20 [shorthand] [51]

22 [shorthand] 23 [shorthand] 24 [shorthand] 25 [shorthand] [47]

GROUP E

21 [shorthand]

GROUP F

26 [shorthand] 27 [shorthand] 28 [shorthand] 29 [shorthand] [29]

Principles

26 Alphabet Review

Here are all the shorthand letters you studied in Lessons 1 through 4. See how rapidly you can read them.

27 A, Ä

The large circle that represents the long sound of $\bar{a}$, as in *main*, also represents the vowel sounds heard in *as* and *park*.

A

as, a-s	last, l-a-s-t	happy, h-a-p-e
had, h-a-d	plan, p-l-a-n	man, m-a-n

Ä

park, p-a-r-k	car, k-a-r	far, f-a-r
mark, m-a-r-k	start, s-t-a-r-t	arm, a-r-m

28 E, I, Obscure Vowel

The tiny circle that represents the sound of $\bar{e}$, as in *heat,* also represents the vowel sounds heard in *best, him,* and the obscure vowel sound heard in *her, hurt.*

E

best, b-e-s-t	letter, l-e-t-r	set, s-e-t

help, h-e-l-p

I

him, h-e-m

bill, b-e-l

red, r-e-d

bid, b-e-d

visit, v-e-s-e-t

settle, s-e-t-l

city, s-e-t-e

did, d-e-d

Obscure Vowel

her, h-e-r

first, f-e-r-s-t

serve, s-e-r-v

earn, e-r-n

answer, a-n-s-e-r

hurt, h-e-r-t

29 Th

Two tiny curves, written upward, are provided for the sounds of *th*. These curves are called *ith*.

Over Ith   Under Ith

Over Ith

these, ith-e-s

thick, ith-e-k

then, ith-e-n

bath, b-a-ith

teeth, t-e-ith

smooth, s-m-oo-ith

Under Ith

though, ith-o

those, ith-o-s

three, ith-r-e

earth, e-r-ith

health, h-e-l-ith

clothing, k-l-o-ith-ing

30 Brief Forms

Here is another group of brief forms for very frequently used business words. Learn them well.

is, his

the

that

can

you, your

Mrs.

of

with

but

31 Phrases

Here are useful phrases formed with some of these brief forms.

in the	⌒	*with you*	◠	*do you*	⌇
of the	✓	*you can*	⌒	*you have*	⌇
with the	◠	*I cannot*	⌒	*you are*	⌒

● Reading Practice

Your progress has been so rapid that you can already read business letters written entirely in shorthand.

32 Brief-Form Letter

This letter contains one or more illustrations of all the brief forms in this lesson.

[74]

33

[74]

34

[73]

35

[68]

RECALL

Lesson 6 is a "breather." It contains no new strokes for you to learn. In this lesson you will find an Alphabet Review, a simple explanation of the principles that govern the joining of the strokes you studied in Lessons 1 through 5, a Recall Chart, and a Reading Practice employing the shorthand devices of Lessons 1 through 5.

36 Alphabet Review

Here are the shorthand strokes you studied thus far. Can you read them in 20 seconds or less?

Principles of Joining

As a matter of interest, you might like to know the principles by which the words you have already learned are written. Notice the groups into which the joinings naturally fall.

37 Circles are written inside curves and outside angles.

appear,
a-p-e-r

relieve,
r-e-l-e-v

given,
gay-e-v-n

needless,
n-e-d-l-e-s

decrease,
d-e-k-r-e-s

favors,
f-a-v-r-s

38 Circles are written clockwise (in this direction ↻) on a straight line or between two straight strokes in the same direction.

me, m-e

aim, a-m

may, m-a

mean, m-e-n

man, m-a-n

stayed, s-t-a-d

39 Between two curves written in opposite directions, the circle is written on the back of the first curve.

gear, gay-e-r ~~ wreck, r-e-k ~~ pave, p-a-v ~~

care, k-a-r ~~ leg, l-e-gay ~~ vapor, v-a-p-r ~~

40 The o hook is written on its side before n, m unless a downward character comes before the hook.

owns, o-n-s ~~ loan, l-o-n ~~ homes, h-o-m-s ~~

but

bone, b-o-n ~~ zone, s-o-n ~~ phone, f-o-n ~~

41 The oo hook is written on its side after n, m.

news, n-oo-s ~~ noon, n-oo-n ~~ moved, m-oo-v-d ~~

42 The over ith is used in most words, but when ith is joined to o, r, l, the under ith is used.

these, ith-e-s ~~ both, b-o-ith ~~ throw, ith-r-o ~~

43 Recall Chart

The following chart reviews the shorthand devices you studied in Lessons 1 through 5. It is divided into three parts: words, brief forms, and phrases.

Spell each word aloud thus: ith-r-o, throw. You need not spell the brief forms and phrases.

There are 84 shorthand outlines in the chart. Can you read the entire chart in 10 minutes or less?

WORDS

1						
2						
3						
4						

5						
6						

BRIEF FORMS

7						
8						
9						

PHRASES

10						
11						
12						
13						
14						

● **Reading Practice**

44

[75]

45

[84]

46

[80]

47

[69]

Shorthand
A Vital Office Skill

Speedy communications are the heart of every modern business office. To keep business running smoothly, it is absolutely necessary to get information from one location to another quickly and accurately. Shorthand is the first step in the process of recording and transmitting information.

Let's take a peek at the activities in an office on an ordinary business day. We are listening to Mr. Johnson, the national product manager for a large distributor of electronic calculators, and his secretary, Ms. Rubin.

"Ms. Rubin, I have Mr. O'Brien on the phone from Los Angeles. Would you take down the revised specifications he has for the new line of calculators and then come into my office.

"Now, those specifications will have to be incorporated into the report, and copies of the revised report will have to be sent to all the regional managers immediately.

"Get a letter off special delivery to Mrs. Walters in Chicago and ask her to have her top engineer ready to revise the plans as soon as we get the specifications. After she has had a chance to discuss them with the engineer, ask her to let me know how extensive the changes will be.

"Ask Chuck to tell Lee Johnson that the final specs are in and will be ready for the national meeting next week. Make sure to send five copies by tomorrow afternoon.

"Get Albini and Pierce on the phone and tell them that they should be here the day before the meeting so that we can discuss the warehousing problems. I'll pick them up at the airport Monday afternoon.

"Call Mrs. Lopez in public relations and tell her that as soon as she gets the new specs, she can release the national campaign. Ask her if she needs any more pictures of the machine."

All this happened in less than three minutes. If the instructions given are not carried out correctly, many problems could arise. Since the flow of information may be like this all day in an office, these instructions must not be entrusted to memory. So many people and so many facts are involved, it would be too easy to confuse what Mr. Johnson just said. The information should be written. But in that short space of time, how can it all be recorded correctly? The answer is with shorthand!

With the fast pace of business today, everyone who works in an office would benefit from the ability to take shorthand. For a secretary, however, it is a must! Whether working for an accountant or a zoologist, a secretary has to be prepared to listen to, to record, and to act upon an enormous amount of information daily. What office skill could make this task easier than shorthand?

Principles

48 Sh, Ch, J

The shorthand stroke for *sh* (called *ish*) is a very short downward straight stroke.
The shorthand stroke for *ch* (called *chay*) is a longer downward straight stroke approximately half the height of the space between the lines in your shorthand notebook.
The shorthand stroke for the sound of *j*, as in *jail* and *age*, is a long downward straight stroke almost the full height of the space between the lines in your shorthand notebook.

▶ Note carefully the difference in the sizes of these strokes.

Ish / Chay / J /

Ish

she, ish-e	showed, ish-o-d	share, ish-a-r
show, ish-o	ship, ish-e-p	insure, in-ish-oo-r

Chay

each, e-chay	attach, a-t-a-chay	chair, chay-a-r
teach, t-e-chay	church, chay-e-r-chay	check, chay-e-k

J

age, a-j	page, p-a-j	change, chay-a-n-j
large, l-a-r-j	charge, chay-a-r-j	jail, j-a-l

49 O, Aw

The small deep hook that represents the sound of *o*, as in *no*, also represents the vowel sounds heard in *hot* and *all*.

O

hot, h-o-t	lot, l-o-t	stock, s-t-o-k

job, j-o-b

copy, k-o-p-e

college, k-o-l-e-j

sorry, s-o-r-e

top, t-o-p

drop, d-r-o-p

Aw

all, o-l

call, k-o-l

small, s-m-o-l

install, in-s-t-o-l

bought, b-o-t

cause, k-o-s

taught, t-o-t

daughter, d-o-t-r

wall, oo-o-l

50 Common Business Letter Salutations and Closings

Dear Sir

Dear Madam

Yours truly

Sincerely yours

Yours very truly

Very truly yours

▸ Note: While the expressions *Dear Sir, Dear Madam,* and *Yours truly* are considered too impersonal by experts in letter writing, they are still used by many dictators. Therefore, special abbreviations are provided for them.

Building Transcription Skills

51
BUSINESS
VOCABULARY
BUILDER

As a stenographer and secretary, you will constantly be working with words. Consequently, the larger the vocabulary you have at your command, the easier will be your task of taking dictation and transcribing.

To help you build your vocabulary at the same time that you are learning shorthand, a Business Vocabulary Builder is provided in Lesson 7 and in many other lessons that follow. The Business Vocabulary Builder consists of brief definitions of business words and expressions, selected from the Reading and Writing Practice, that should be part of your everyday vocabulary.

Be sure you understand the meaning of the words and expressions before you begin to work on the Reading and Writing Practice of the lesson.

Business
Vocabulary
Builder

vital Very important.

copier A machine for making printed copies.

obligate Bind; commit.

● Reading and Writing Practice

Suggestion Before you begin your work on the letters in this Reading and Writing Practice, turn to page 10 and read the procedures outlined there for reading and writing shorthand. By following those key suggestions you will derive the greatest benefit from your practice.

52 Brief-Form Review Letter

This letter reviews the brief forms you studied in Lessons 3 and 5.

[shorthand outlines] [104]

53 *[shorthand outlines]* [84]

54

18

[83]

55

[51]

56

20 2

1977

[61]

Principles

57 Brief Forms

Here is the third group of brief forms for frequently used words. Learn them well.

for	⟩	this	⌒	which	/
would	/	good	⌒	them	⌒
there (their)	⟋	they	⌒	be,* by	⟨

*Be is also used as a word beginning in words such as *begin* and *believe*.

Spell: be-gay-e-n, begin

| begin | ↳ | believe | ⟨ | because | ⟨ |

58 Word Ending -ly

The common word ending *-ly* is represented by the *e* circle.

Spell: n-e-r-lē, nearly

nearly	⟋	fairly	⟋	sincerely	⟋
only	⟋	properly	⟨	mainly	⟋
early	⟋	mostly	⟋	daily	⟋

▶ Notice that the circle for *ly* in *daily* is added to the other side of the *d* after the *a* has been written.

59 Amounts and Quantities

In business you will frequently have to take dictation in which amounts and quantities are used. Here are some devices that will help you write them rapidly.

400	*4̠*	$4	*4/*	4 o'clock	*4ᵘ*		
4,000	*4,*	$4,000	*4/*	$4.50	*4⁵⁰*		
400,000	*4,*	$400,000	*4/*	4 percent	*4,*		

▶ Notice that the *n* for *hundred* and the *ith* for *thousand* are placed underneath the figure.

Building Transcription Skills

60
Business
Vocabulary
Builder

brochure Booklet.

dry goods Textiles; ready-to-wear clothing.

cassettes Small plastic cartridges containing magnetic tape on reels.

● Reading and Writing Practice

61 Brief-Form Letter

The following letter contains one or more illustrations of the brief forms presented in this lesson.

Principles

65 Word Ending -tion

The word ending *-tion* (also spelled *sion*, *cian*, or *shion*) is represented by *ish*.

Spell: s-e-k-shun, section

section	*ん*	vacation	*ろ*	national	*ℓ*
operation	*ℓ*	occasion	*ら*	fashion	*d*
collection	*∿σ*	nation	*ρ*	physician	*q*

66 Word Endings -cient, -ciency

The word ending *-cient* (or *-tient*) is represented by *ish-t*; *-ciency*, by *ish-s-e*.

Spell: e-f-e-shun-t, efficient

p-r-o-f-e-shun-s-e, proficiency

efficient	*d*	patient	*6*	proficiency	*Cy*

67 T for To in Phrases

In phrases, *to* is represented by *t* when it is followed by a downstroke.

to be	*1*	to plan	*ℓ*	to place	*ℓ*
to have	*1*	to fill	*2*	to see	*6*
to pay	*6*	to check	*2*	to say	*6*

Building Transcription Skills

68
Business Vocabulary Builder

authorize To give permission to.

staggering Alternating.

sectional Local; regional.

collection agency An organization that collects past-due accounts.

● Reading and Writing Practice

69 Brief-Form Review Letter

The following letter reviews the brief forms in Lesson 8 as well as many of the brief forms in Lessons 3 and 5.

[shorthand notes] [100]

70

[shorthand notes]

[93]

71

15

5

15

15

15

[107]

72

1977

62

15

[93]

Principles

73 Nd

The shorthand strokes for *n-d* are joined without an angle to form the *nd* blend, as in *trained*.

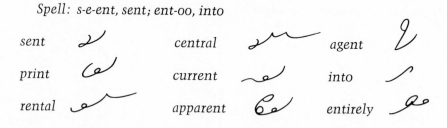

Nd

Compare: train   trained

Spell: *t-r-a-end, trained*

signed		land		friend	
assigned		planned		spend	
find		kind		lined	

74 Nt

The stroke that represents *nd* also represents *nt*, as in *sent*.

Spell: *s-e-ent, sent; ent-oo, into*

sent		central		agent	
print		current		into	
rental		apparent		entirely	

75 Ses

The sound of *ses*, as in *senses*, is represented by joining the two forms of *s*.

Compare: sense   senses

face   faces

Spell: s-e-n-sez, senses

senses	services	necessary
processes	offices	promises

76 Sis, Sus

The similar sounds of *sis*, as in *sister*, and *sus*, as in *versus*, are also represented by joining the two forms of *s*.

Spell: sez-t-r, sister; v-e-r-sez, versus

sister	basis	assist
analysis	insist	versus

Building Transcription Skills

77
Business
Vocabulary
Builder

processes *(noun)* Methods; procedures.

went astray Lost.

current Most recent.

● Reading and Writing Practice

78 Brief-Form Review Letter

This letter reviews all the brief forms you studied in Lesson 8.

[73]

79

[Gregg shorthand outlines] (50,

[shorthand outlines] [98]

80

[shorthand outlines] 8

) 240/ 2

[shorthand outlines] 15,

[shorthand outlines] [64]

81

[shorthand outlines]) 240/

[shorthand outlines]) 240/

18

25

[Shorthand outlines — paragraph 94]

[Shorthand outlines — paragraph 82, ending 48]

83 [Shorthand outlines, ending 76]

SHORTHAND READING CHECKLIST

When you read shorthand, do you—

- 1 Read aloud so that you know that you are concentrating on each outline that you read?
- 2 Spell each outline that you cannot immediately read?
- 3 Reread each Reading and Writing Practice a second time?
- 4 Occasionally reread the suggestions for reading shorthand given on pages 10 and 11?

Principles

84 Brief Forms

and	/	*should*	✓	*after*	𝓺
when	⌐	*could*	⌐	*street*	𝓷
from	𝓛	*send*	𝓳	*were*	𝓮

85 Rd

The combination *rd* is represented by writing *r* with an upward turn at the finish.

Compare: *answer* ⟋⟍   *answered* ⟋⟍

Spell: *a-n-s-e-ärd, answered; h-e-ärd, heard*

prepared		*heard*	⟍	*record*	⌐⟍
assured	𝓮𝓱	*hard*	⟍	*recorded*	⌐⟍
ignored	⟋⟍	*harder*	⟍	*toward*	⟍

86 Ld

The combination *ld* is represented by writing the *l* with an upward turn at the finish.

Compare: *call* ⟍   *called* ⟍

Spell: *k-o-eld, called; o-eld, old*

called	⟍	*failed*	⟍	*children*	𝓮
held	⟍	*old*	⟍	*billed*	𝓮
child	𝓮	*told*	⟍	*folded*	𝓛

87 Been in Phrases

The word *been* is represented by *b* after *have, has, had.*

had been   *(shorthand)*   I have been   *(shorthand)*   it has been   *(shorthand)*

have been   *(shorthand)*   I have not been   *(shorthand)*   should have been   *(shorthand)*

88 Able in Phrases

The word *able* is represented by *a* after *be* or *been.*

have been able   *(shorthand)*   has been able   *(shorthand)*

I have been able   *(shorthand)*   I should be able   *(shorthand)*

you have not been able   *(shorthand)*   you will be able   *(shorthand)*

Building Transcription Skills

89
Business Vocabulary Builder

plight Bad state or condition.
asset Advantage.
"on the drawing boards" In the planning stage.
ignored Neglected.

● Reading and Writing Practice

90 Brief-Form Letter

The following letter contains one or more illustrations of every brief form in paragraph 84.

(shorthand outlines)

[114]

91

[115]

92

[92]

93

[77]

94

95

1975

[65]

[56]

RECALL

Lesson 12 is another "breather" for you; it presents no new shorthand devices for you to learn. It contains a number of principles of joining, a helpful Recall Chart, and several short letters that you should have no difficulty reading.

Principles of Joining

96 At the beginning and end of words, the comma *s* is used before and after *f, v, k, g;* the left *s*, before and after *p, b, r, l.*

safes		globes		sales	
sips		scares		rags	

97 The comma *s* is used before *t, d, n, m, o;* the left *s* is used after those characters.

stones		solos		needs	
smart		meets		seed	

98 The comma *s* is used before and after *ish, chay, j.*

sashes		reaches		stages	

99 The comma *s* is used in words consisting of an *s* and a circle vowel or *s* and *ith* and a circle vowel.

see		these		seethe	

100 Gregg Shorthand is equally legible whether it is written on ruled or unruled paper; consequently you need not worry about the exact placement of your outlines on the printed lines in your notebook. You will be able to read your outlines regardless of their placement on the printed line. The main purpose that the printed lines in your notebook serve is to keep you from wandering uphill and downhill as you write.

However, so that all outlines may be uniformly placed in the shorthand books from which you study, this general rule has been followed:

The base of the first consonant of a word is placed on the line of writing. When *s* comes before a downstroke, however, the downstroke is placed on the line of writing.

| *dealer* | | *names* | | *pays* | |
| *save* | | *chief* | | *space* | |

101 Recall Chart

The following chart contains all the brief forms presented in Chapter 2 and one or more illustrations of the shorthand principles you studied in Chapters 1 and 2.

Can you read the entire chart in 9 minutes or less?

BRIEF FORMS

1					
2					
3					

PHRASES AND AMOUNTS

4					
5					
6					
7					

WORDS

8					
9					
10					
11					

12	◠	◠	◠◡	◠◡	◡	◡◡
13	ﻭ	ﻭ	ﻭ	ﻭ	ﻭ	ﻭ
14	◡	◡	ﻭ	ﻭ	◡	◡

Building Transcription Skills

102

Business Vocabulary Builder

fee A charge.

leaflet A single printed sheet of paper.

glowing Showing elation or great satisfaction.

● Reading and Writing Practice

103

[113]

104

106

[89]

[82]

105

[69]

The
Secretarial Profession
A Brief History

The Bettmann Archive

The word *secretary* is derived from the Latin meaning "secret" or "one who is entrusted with secrets." The earliest records of ancient civilizations indicate that scribes were used by the Assyrians as long ago as the eighteenth century B.C., and by the Romans in the eighth century B.C. By the second century B.C., scribes had reached professional status and were employed in the libraries of Alexandria to compile materials for Rome's first public libraries. By the fourth century A.D., scribes were used to assist with the business affairs and personal correspondence of those who could not read and write. Most affairs of government also required the services of scribes, then called secretary-scribes.

Toward the end of the nineteenth century, with the invention of the typewriter and the Gregg Shorthand system, many women became proficient in secretarial work and began to take over duties formerly performed by men. These "type-writers," as secretaries were then called, were trailblazers in business offices. They were eager to trade a life on the farm or in the factory for a very different life in a business office. Although their manner was quiet; their role, subservient; their dress, conservative; their pay, meager, the historical impact of these women was revolutionary. They were instrumental in changing the whole character of the business office. Today there are several million secretaries in the United States. Though the majority are women, many men are now choosing this as their profession. Secretaries' titles range from junior stenographer to administrative assistant; their work, from taking shorthand and transcribing verbatim notes on the typewriter to handling all administrative duties of a large modern business organization. Secretaries may work in many different kinds of places, from small, one-secretary offices to large communications centers in major cities. They may work for many executives or for only one. But their function is basically the same—keeping business running smoothly through the application of their secretarial skills and abilities.

The status of today's secretary ranks considerably higher than the status of a secretary 50 years ago. The secretary is really an executive aide who still does the traditional jobs of taking dictation, typing, filing, and handling calls and callers. But in many ways, today's secretary must know the job of the boss better than the boss does.

It has been said that behind every good executive there's a good secretary. Today there is a tremendous demand for good secretaries, and authoritative sources indicate that this demand will continue to grow. The secretary is an established and vital part of the structure of modern business.

Principles

107 Brief Forms

glad	⌣	circular	6	enclose	⌣
work	⌣	order	✓	was	૮
yesterday	𝒴	soon	∠	thank*	⌒

*In phrases, the dot is omitted from *thank*. *Thanks* is written with a disjoined left *s* in the dot position.

thank you	⌒	thank you for	ʒ	thanks	⌒

108 U, OO

The hook that represents the sound of *oo*, as in *to*, also represents the vowel sounds heard in *does* and *book*.

U

Spell: d-oo-s, does

does	β	enough	ʒ	us	⁊
drug	⌒	number	⌒	just	⅃
product	⌒	must	⌒	precious	⌒

▶ Notice: ■ 1 The hook in *enough*, *number*, and *must* is turned on its side;

■ 2 *oo-s* in *us*, *just*, *precious* join without an angle.

oo

Spell: b-oo-k, book

book	⟋	full	⟋	took	⟋
put	⟋	cook	⟋	foot	⟋
pull	⟋	push	⟋	sugar	⟋

Building Transcription Skills

**109
Business
Vocabulary
Builder**

promotion pieces Circulars or bulletins advertising a company's products.

sketches Rough drawings.

major Greater in importance.

● Reading and Writing Practice

110 Brief-Form Letter

All the brief forms in this lesson, or their derivatives, are used in this letter.

[shorthand outlines]

[98]

111

[shorthand outlines]

15/

450/

[98]

113

480/

15/

[78]

[101]

112

30

480/

114

[shorthand outlines]

[66]

115

[shorthand outlines]

[109]

UP-AND-DOWN CHECKLIST

Do you always write the following strokes upward?

■ 1 and [outline]   their (there) [outline]   ■ 2 it-at [outline]   would [outline]

Do you always write the following strokes downward?

■ 1 is-his [outline]   for [outline]   have [outline]   ■ 2 she [outline]   which [outline]

Principles

116 W in the Body of a Word

When the sound of *w* occurs in the body of a word, as in *quick,* it is represented by a short dash underneath the vowel following the *w* sound. The dash is inserted after the rest of the outline has been written.

Spell: k-oo-e-k, quick

quick		between		qualify	
quit		square		always	
quote		hardware		Broadway	

117 Ted

The combination *ted* is represented by joining *t* and *d* into one long upward stroke.

Ted

Compare: heat   heed   heated

Spell: h-e-ted, heated

listed		quoted		rested	
drafted		tested		steady	
acted		accepted		today	

118 Ded

The long stroke that represents *ted* also represents *ded* and the similar sounds of *dit*, *det*.

Spell: *gay-ī-ded, guided; det-a-l, detail*

Ded

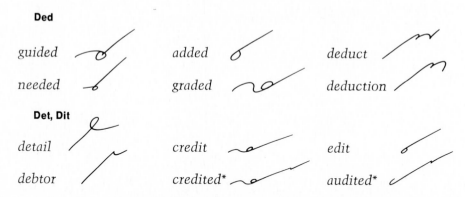

guided		added		deduct	
needed		graded		deduction	

Det, Dit

detail		credit		edit	
debtor		credited*		audited*	

▶ *Notice that the *d* representing the past tense is joined to *det* with a jog.

Building Transcription Skills

119
Business
Vocabulary
Builder

drafted Made a rough copy of.

applicant One who applies for a job.

fine arts Music, literature, painting, etc.

● Reading and Writing Practice

120 Brief-Form Review Letter

This letter reviews all the brief forms you studied in Lesson 13 as well as many from earlier lessons.

[78]

121

[134]

122

123

[66]

15 [90]

124

125

116–1188 [139]

23

25

25

10

39

Principles

126 Brief Forms

value	what	business
than	about	doctor
one (won)	thing, think	any

127 Brief-Form Derivatives

once	thinking	businessman
things, thinks	anything	businesses

▶ Notice that a disjoined left *s* is used to express *things, thinks;* that the plural of *business* is formed by adding a left *s.*

128 Word Ending -ble

The word ending *-ble* is represented by *b.*

Spell: p-o-s-bul, possible

possible	available	table
capable	favorable	trouble
reliable	sensible	troubled

129 Word Beginning Re-

The word beginning *re-* is represented by *r*.

Spell: re-s-e-v, receive

receive	*(outline)*	resigned	*(outline)*	reasonable	*(outline)*
replace	*(outline)*	reception	*(outline)*	reappear	*(outline)*
research	*(outline)*	repairs	*(outline)*	reopen	*(outline)*

Building Transcription Skills

130
Business Vocabulary Builder

queries Questions.

resigned Quit; gave up one's position.

patient *(adjective)* Bearing pains or trials without complaint.

● Reading and Writing Practice

131 Brief-Form Letter

All the brief forms in Lesson 15, or derivatives of them, are used at least once in this letter.

(shorthand outlines)

[118]

132

[Shorthand content]

150/

133

[Shorthand content]

[122]

[96]

134

135

136

[81]

[84]

[76]

Principles

137 Oi

The sound of *oi*, as in *toy*, is represented by ↻ .

Spell: t-oi, toy

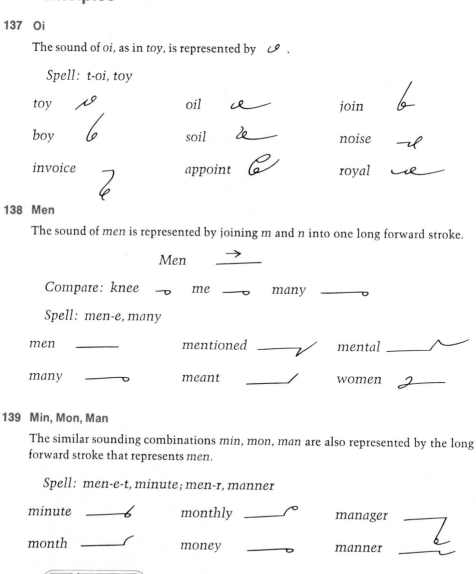

toy	oil	join
boy	soil	noise
invoice	appoint	royal

138 Men

The sound of *men* is represented by joining *m* and *n* into one long forward stroke.

Men →

Compare: knee ⟿ me ⟿ many ⟿

Spell: men-e, many

men	mentioned	mental
many	meant	women

139 Min, Mon, Man

The similar sounding combinations *min, mon, man* are also represented by the long forward stroke that represents *men*.

Spell: men-e-t, minute; men-r, manner

minute	monthly	manager
month	money	manner

140 Ye, Ya

Ye, as in *year,* is represented by the *e* circle; *ya,* as in *yard,* by the *a* circle.

Spell: *e-r, year; a-ärd, yard*

Ye

year	‍	yes	9	yield	
yet		yellow		yielded	

Ya

yard		yarn		Yale	

Building Transcription Skills

141

Business Vocabulary Builder

craftsmen Workers who practice a trade or handicraft.

net profit Amount remaining after the deduction of expenses.

sizable Fairly large; considerable.

decade Ten years.

● Reading and Writing Practice

142 Brief-Form Review Letter

This letter reviews all the brief forms you studied in Lesson 15 as well as many from earlier lessons.

[shorthand notation]

[105]

143

[81]

144

[90]

145

147

[47]

[104]

146

250/

[65]

Principles

148 Brief Forms

When you have learned the following brief forms, you will have learned more than half the brief forms of Gregg Shorthand.

gentlemen		where		next	
important, importance		company		short	
morning		manufacture			

149 Word Beginnings Per-, Pur-

The word beginnings *per-, pur-* are represented by *p-r.*

Spell: pur-s-n, person; pur-chay-a-s, purchase

Per-

person		perhaps		perfect	
personal		permanent		permit	

Pur-

purchase		purpose		purple	

150 Word Beginnings De-, Di-

The word beginnings *de-, di-* are represented by *d.*

Spell: de-s-ī-d, decide; de-r-e-k-t, direct

De-

decide depend deliver

decision deposit desire

Di-

direct direction director

Building Transcription Skills

151
SIMILAR-WORDS
DRILL

The English language contains many groups of words that sound or look alike, but each member of the group may be spelled differently and have its own meaning.

Example: **sent** (dispatched); **scent** (a smell); **cent** (a coin).

In addition, there are many groups of words that sound or look *almost* alike.

Example: **area** (space); **aria** (a melody).

The stenographer or secretary who is not alert may, while transcribing, select the wrong member of the group, with the result that the transcript makes no sense.

In this lesson and in a number of others that follow, you will find a Similar-Words Drill that will call to your attention common groups of similar words on which a careless stenographer might stumble.

Study each definition carefully and read the illustrative examples. These similar words are used in the letters of the Reading and Writing Practice exercises.

SIMILAR-WORDS
DRILL
personal, personnel

personal Individual; private; pertaining to the person or body.

Harry is a personal *friend of mine.*
Do you watch your personal *appearance with care?*

personnel The people who work for a firm; the staff.

Our personnel *will take care of your needs.*
Mr. Green is the personnel *director of our firm.*

purchasing agent A person responsible for purchasing goods or supplies for a company.

proceed To move ahead.

anticipated Expected.

● Reading and Writing Practice

153 **Brief-Form Letter**

[shorthand outlines]

[153]

154

[shorthand outlines]

155

156

[116]

[107]

[102]

157

[116]

[70]

158

[74]

159

[70]

LESSON 18

RECALL

Lesson 18 contains no new shorthand devices for you to learn. In this lesson you will find: (1) a number of additional principles of joining, (2) a Recall Chart, and (3) a Reading and Writing Practice that you will find not only interesting but informative as well.

Principles of Joining

160 At the beginning of a word and after *k*, *g*, or a downstroke, the combination *oo-s* is written without an angle.

husky   *shorthand*   gust   *shorthand*   just   *shorthand*

but

does   *shorthand*   loose   *shorthand*   rust   *shorthand*

161 The word beginning *re-* is represented by *r* before a downstroke or a vowel.

revised   *shorthand*   reference   *shorthand*   reopen   *shorthand*

but

retake   *shorthand*   remake   *shorthand*   relate   *shorthand*

162 The word beginnings *de-*, *di-* are represented by *d* except before *k* or *g*.

deserving   *shorthand*   depressed   *shorthand*   direct   *shorthand*

but

declare   *shorthand*   decay   *shorthand*   degrade   *shorthand*

163 As you have perhaps already noticed from your study of Lessons 1 through 17, the past tense of a verb is formed by adding the stroke for the sound that is heard in the past tense. In some words, the past tense will have the sound of *t*, as in *baked*; in others, it will have the sound of *d*, as in *saved*.

baked   missed   faced

saved   changed   showed

164 Recall Chart

The following chart reviews the brief forms of Chapter 3 as well as the shorthand principles you studied in Chapters 1, 2, and 3. The chart contains 96 outlines. Can you read it in 9 minutes or less?

BRIEF FORMS

PHRASES AND AMOUNTS

WORDS

14	⟋⟍	⟋⟍⟋	⟋.	⟋⟍	⟋	⟋.
15	⟋	⟋	⟋	⟋	⟋	⟋
16	⟋	⟋	⟋	⟋	⟋	⟋

Building Transcription Skills

165
Business Vocabulary Builder

adjacent Nearby; close to.

primary Of first importance.

routine Ordinary.

● Reading and Writing Practice

Reading Scoreboard One of the factors in measuring shorthand growth is the rate at which you can read shorthand. Here is an opportunity for you to measure your reading speed on the *first reading* of the material in Lesson 18. The following table will help you determine how rapidly you can read shorthand.

Lesson 18 contains 447 words

If you read Lesson 18 in **17 minutes** your reading rate is **26 words a minute**

If you read Lesson 18 in **19 minutes** your reading rate is **24 words a minute**

If you read Lesson 18 in **21 minutes** your reading rate is **21 words a minute**

If you read Lesson 18 in **25 minutes** your reading rate is **18 words a minute**

If you read Lesson 18 in **29 minutes** your reading rate is **16 words a minute**

If you read Lesson 18 in **33 minutes** your reading rate is **14 words a minute**

If you can read Lesson 18 through the first time in less than 17 minutes, you are doing well indeed. If you take considerably longer than 33 minutes, here are some questions you should ask yourself.

■ 1 Am I spelling each outline I cannot read immediately?

■ 2 Am I spending too much time deciphering an outline that I cannot read even after spelling it?

■ 3 Should I perhaps reread the directions for reading shorthand on page 10?

After you have determined your reading rate, make a record of it in some convenient place. You can then watch your reading rate grow as you time yourself on the Reading Scoreboards in later lessons.

[shorthand notation]

On occasion, *[shorthand notation]*

[shorthand notation] 13 19 *[shorthand notation]*

The Importance of Marketing. *[shorthand notation]*

(shorthand outline)

Selling goods *(shorthand outlines)*

[347]

[100]

CHAPTER

What Does the Secretary Do?

A secretary is an administrative assistant who has a mastery of office skills, who assumes responsibility, who works without direct supervision, and who exercises initiative and judgment.

The specific duties of the secretary depend largely upon the nature of the employer's business and the amount of responsibility delegated by the immediate superior.

Usually the secretary handles a variety of business details independently, in addition to stenographic duties. One important aspect of the secretary's job is to represent the employer to the public and to other business people. And it is the secretary who relieves the boss of routine duties, supervises clerical workers, handles correspondence, and records confidential material.

The secretary receives, sorts, and opens mail directed to the employer. Letters marked "Personal" may or may not be opened, depending upon the employer's instructions. The secretary, being the one most familiar with the employer's business practices, may answer much of the mail without supervision. Mail that requires the employer's personal attention is classified for convenience. The boss may either dictate replies or ask the secretary to answer the correspondence according to instructions.

In many instances, the secretary answers inquiries, obtains information, and refers calls to other departments or personnel without disturbing the employer. Many secretaries act as "buffers" by screening all visitors and callers before scheduling appointments. The secretary may take notes at meetings, office conferences, or large meetings. The secretary may also transcribe the reports of the meeting and handle the distribution of copies. In some offices, the secretary supervises other office personnel and assigns work to typists and other clerical workers.

The secretary must be thoroughly familiar with the filing system in order to retrieve information at a moment's notice. The secretary must be able to make travel arrangements and reservations for the employer's business trips and schedule luncheon or dinner dates with clients or customers. The secretary may also be required to take care of the employer's personal business files, business bank account, and business income tax records.

Other duties depend upon the secretary's specialization. A social secretary, for example, would be responsible for arranging social functions, sending invitations, keeping the employer informed of social activities, and answering personal correspondence. A legal secretary should know and be able to use legal terminology.

A technical secretary employed by engineers, chemists, or biologists should understand scientific terms and be able to transcribe highly technical dictation.

Although a secretary's duties vary widely from position to position, the mark of every superior secretary is the ability to assume responsibility and do high-quality work without direct supervision.

Principles

168 Brief Forms

Here is another group of brief forms—only six this time.

present	C	advertise		immediate	
part	C	Ms.		opportunity	$\mathcal{E}$

169 U

The sound of *u*, as in *use*, is represented by σ .

Spell: u-s, use

use		review		united	
few		unit		unique	

170 Word Ending -ment

The word ending -*ment* is represented by *m*.

Spell: p-a-ment, payment

payment		appointment		advertisement	
management		refreshment		department	
arrangement		shipment		assignment	

▶ Notice that in *assignment*, *m* for *ment* is joined to the *n* with a jog.

171 Word Ending -tial (-cial)

The word ending *-tial* is represented by *ish*.

Spell: e-n-e-shul, initial

initial	*of*	social		especially	
initialed		special		financial	
initially		partial		official	

Building Transcription Skills

172
SPELLING

When you look at the letter on page 96, you get a favorable impression. The letter is nicely placed; the right-hand margin is even; the date, inside address, and closing are all in their proper places. When you read the letter casually, it makes good sense and apparently represents what the dictator said.

But that favorable impression vanishes when you read the letter carefully. In fact, the dictator will never sign it because it contains several misspelled words. No executive will knowingly sign a letter that contains a misspelled word!

If you are to succeed as a stenographer or secretary, your letters must not only be accurate transcripts of what your employer dictated but they must also be free of spelling errors. A stenographer or secretary who regularly submits letters for signature that contain spelling errors will not long be welcome in a business office.

To make sure that you will be able to spell correctly when you have completed your shorthand course, you will from this point on give special attention to spelling in each Reading and Writing Practice.

As you read the Reading and Writing Practice, you will occasionally find shorthand outlines printed in a second color. These outlines represent words that transcribers often misspell. When you encounter such an outline, finish reading the sentence in which it occurs; then glance at the margin, where you will find the word in type, properly syllabicated.

Spell the word aloud if possible, pausing slightly after each word division. (The word divisions indicated are those given in *Webster's New Collegiate Dictionary*.)

173
Business Vocabulary Builder

board of trustees A group of people who direct a company's work.

unique Unusual; one of a kind.

prospective Likely to become.

LUNN

CHARLOTTE

COLUMBUS

DENVER

DUBUQUE

ELGIN

FLINT

FT. WAYNE

FT. WORTH

HUNTINGTON

LEXINGTON

MADISON

MEMPHIS

NASHVILLE

NORFOLK

PORTLAND

ST. LOUIS

ST. PAUL

SANTA FE

SAVANNAH

SEATTLE

TEXARKANA

TUCSON

TULSA

WICHITA

September 22, 19--

Mr. John Case
2001 Huron Street
Seattle, Washington 98117

Dear Mr. Case:

It is a comfortible feeling to know that the heating system in your home does not have to depend on the elements. Snow and ice cannot leave you shiverring when you heat with gas. It travels under ground.

The dependability of gas is only one of its many virtues. A gas heating system costs less to instal and less to operate. It needs lots less serviceing, and it lasts longer. It has no odor and makes no filmy deposits that cause extra work.

No wonder more than 400,000 users of other feuls changed to gas last year.

Why not let us show you how easy it is to instal gas heat in your home.

Yours truely,

Thomas A. Frost
Sales Manager

TAF:re

Can you find all the errors in this letter?

● Reading and Writing Practice

174 Brief-Form Letter

[Shorthand outlines]

ap·pli·cants

di·rec·tor

as·sign·ment

de·sir·able

[152]

175

im·me·di·ate·ly

valu·able

through

[148]

176

re·fer·ring [shorthand outline]

be·gin·ning [shorthand outline]

va·can·cies [shorthand outline]

[101]

177

pur·chase [shorthand outline]

[shorthand outlines]

than [shorthand outline]

per·son·al·ly [shorthand outline]

[81]

178

men's [shorthand outline]

suf·fi·cient [shorthand outline]

[50]

Principles

179 Ow

The sound *ow*, as in *now*, is written   ✑ .

   Spell: n-ow, now

now		how		announce	
found		house		south	
account		amount		crowd	

180 Word Ending -ther

The word ending *-ther* is represented by *ith*.

   Spell: oo-ther, other

other		mother		either	
another		gather		leather	
whether		gathered		bothered	

181 Word Beginning Con-

The word beginning *con-* is represented by *k*.

   Spell: con-s-e-r-n, concern

concern		considerable		consisted	
concrete		control		contract	

182 Word Beginning Com-

The word beginning *com-* is also represented by *k*.

Spell: com-p-l-e-t, complete

complete	compare	complain
computer	combine	compliment

183 Con-, Com- Followed by a Vowel

When con-, com- are followed by a vowel, these word beginnings are represented by *kn* or *km*.

connect   committee   commercial

Building Transcription Skills

184
Business
Vocabulary
Builder

compliment *(verb)* To express a favorable comment.

comptrollers Persons who supervise the financial affairs of a business.

utilized Made use of.

comprehensive Covering completely or broadly.

● Reading and Writing Practice

185 Brief-Form Review Letter

com·pli·ment

caught

118

com·put·er

comp·trol·lers

fi·nan·cial

[109]

[110]

186

re·ceived

past

crowd·ed

oc·cu·py

187

nec·es·sary

com·pa·nies

per·son·nel

com·pli·men·ta·ry

[118]

188

[shorthand outlines]

wheth·er

[shorthand outlines]

rec·om·mend

ad·vice

[101]

189

[shorthand outlines]

cou·pon

con·trac·tors

[65]

Principles

190 Brief Forms

advantage .... *(outline)*   several .... *(outline)*   ever, every .... *(outline)*

suggest .... *(outline)*   out .... *(outline)*   very .... *(outline)*

191 Ten

By rounding off the angle between *t-n*, we obtain the fluent *ten* blend.

Ten *(outline)*

Spell: *a-ten-d, attend; k-o-ten, cotton*

attend .... *(outline)*   remittance .... *(outline)*   bulletin .... *(outline)*

attention .... *(outline)*   stand .... *(outline)*   cotton .... *(outline)*

written .... *(outline)*   standard .... *(outline)*   button .... *(outline)*

tennis .... *(outline)*   assistance .... *(outline)*   tonight .... *(outline)*

192 Den

The stroke that represents *ten* also represents *d-n*.

Spell: *e-v-den-t, evident*

evident .... *(outline)*   president .... *(outline)*   dentist .... *(outline)*

student .... *(outline)*   deny .... *(outline)*   danger .... *(outline)*

confident .... *(outline)*   sudden .... *(outline)*   dinner .... *(outline)*

193 Tain

The stroke that represents *t-n, d-n* also represents *-tain.*

Spell: o-b-tain, obtain

obtain	certain	obtainable
maintain	attain	container

Building Transcription Skills

194
**Business
Vocabulary
Builder**

remittance Money sent to someone.

creditors Persons to whom money is owed.

browse To look over casually.

reproduced Made a copy of.

● Reading and Writing Practice

195 Brief-Form Letter

re·mit·tance

es·caped

ad·van·tage

los·ing

[125]

196

cat·a·log

browse

wom·en's

equip·ment

con·fi·dent

[147]

197

cop·ies

as·sis·tance

ap·prov·al

[130]

198

as·sis·tant

[Shorthand notes]

sal·a·ry

than

[89]

[62]

ac·cept·ed

STUDY-HABIT CHECKLIST *No doubt as a conscientious student you do your home assignments faithfully. Do you, however, derive the greatest benefit from the time you devote to practice?*

- *You do* if you practice in a quiet place that enables you to concentrate.
- *You don't* if you practice with one eye on the television and the other on your practice work!
- *You do* if once you have started your assignment, you do not leave your desk or table until you have completed it.
- *You don't* if you interrupt your practice from time to time to call a friend or raid the refrigerator!

Principles

200 Tem

By rounding off the angle between *t-m*, we obtain the fluent *tem* blend.

Tem

Compare: ten   tem

Spell: tem-p-l, temple

temple	attempt	estimate
temporary	item	customer
system	tomorrow	automobile

201 Dem

The stroke that represents *tem* also represents *d-m*.

Spell: dem-a-end, demand

demand	damage	seldom
demonstrate	domestic	medium

202 Business Abbreviations

Here are additional salutations and closings frequently used in business.

Dear Mr.	Dear Ms.	Yours sincerely
Dear Mrs.	Dear Miss	Cordially yours

203 Useful Phrases

With the *ten* and *tem* blends, we form these useful phrases:

to me 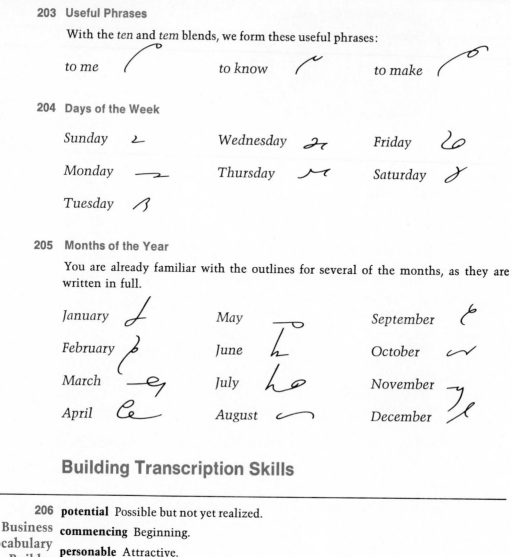   to know   to make

204 Days of the Week

Sunday   Wednesday   Friday

Monday   Thursday   Saturday

Tuesday

205 Months of the Year

You are already familiar with the outlines for several of the months, as they are written in full.

January   May   September

February   June   October

March   July   November

April   August   December

Building Transcription Skills

206
Business Vocabulary Builder

potential Possible but not yet realized.

commencing Beginning.

personable Attractive.

● Reading and Writing Practice

207 Brief-Form Review Letter

po·ten·tial

sim·ply

col·or

[118]

208

an·noy·ance

per·ma·nent

com·menc·ing

in·ci·den·tal·ly

routes

[131]

209

350/

16 =

sur·prised

50,

enough

pro·ceed

[120]

210

Feb·ru·ary
too

launched

sim·i·lar

× ac

[104]

211

sup·plies

shipped

[67]

Principles

212 Brief Forms

After this group, you have only four more groups to learn.

time		general		organize	
acknowledge		question		over*	

*The outline for *over* is written above the following character. It is also used as a prefix form, as in:

overdue   overcame   oversee

213 Def, Dif

By rounding off the angle between *d-f*, we obtain the fluent *def, dif* blend.

Def, Dif

Spell: def-n-e-t, definite

definite		defeat		different	
definitely		defend		differences	

214 Div, Dev

The stroke that represents *def, dif* also represents *div* and *dev*.

Spell: div-ī-d, divide

divide		develop		devote	
division		devised		devoted	

215 Ea, Ia

The sound of *ea*, as in *create* and *piano*, is represented by a large circle with a dot placed within it.

Spell: k-r-eah-t, create

create	appreciate	brilliant
piano	appropriate	area

Building Transcription Skills

216
SIMILAR-WORDS
DRILL
to, too, two

to *(preposition)* In the direction of. *(To* is also used as the sign of the infinitive.)

I would like to talk to you about this matter.

too Also; more than enough.

I, too, am free on that day.
Harry has too many irons in the fire.

two One plus one.

James bought two new suits.

   The word in this group on which many stenographers stumble is *too.* They carelessly transcribe *to.* Don't make that mistake.

217
Business
Vocabulary
Builder

media *(plural of* medium) Channels of communication.

contemplate Consider.

associate *(noun)* Partner; colleague.

merge To combine into one.

● Reading and Writing Practice

218 Brief-Form Letter

[Shorthand outlines fill the page, arranged in two columns divided by a vertical line.]

ac·knowl·edge

re·ferred

me·dia

rev·e·nue

re·cent·ly

[200]

219

ac·knowl·edged

mod·el

bril·liant

every day

(shorthand outlines)

guar·an·tee

[147]

220

as·so·ci·ate

an·swer

too

15

[120]

221

bears

1853

show·rooms

[104]

RECALL

In Lesson 24 you will have no new shorthand devices to learn; you will have a little time to "digest" the devices that you have studied in previous lessons. In Lesson 24 you will find a new feature—Accuracy Practice—that will help you improve your shorthand writing style.

Accuracy Practice

The speed and accuracy with which you will be able to transcribe your shorthand notes will depend on how well you write them. If you follow the suggestions given in this lesson when you work with each Accuracy Practice, you will soon find that you can read your own notes with greater ease and facility.

So that you may have a clear picture of the proper shapes of the shorthand strokes that you are studying, enlarged models of the alphabetic characters and of the typical joinings are given, together with a short explanation of the things that you should keep in mind as you practice.

To get the most out of each Accuracy Practice, follow this simple procedure:

- a *Read the explanations carefully.*
- b *Study the model to see the application of each explanation.*
- c *Write the first outline in the Practice Drill.*
- d *Compare what you have written with the enlarged model.*
- e *Write three or four more copies of the outline, trying to improve your outline with each writing.*
- f *Repeat this procedure with the remaining outlines in the Practice Drill.*

222   **R**   **L**   **K**   **Gay**

To write these strokes accurately:

- a *Start and finish each one on the same level of writing.*

■ b *Make the* beginning *of the curve in* r *and* l *deep. Make the* end *of the curve in* k *and* gay *deep.*

■ c *Make the* l *and* gay *considerably longer than* r *and* k

practice drill

Are-our-hour; will-well; can, good.
Air, lay, ache, gay.

223   **K-r**   **R-k**   **Gay-l**

To write these combinations accurately:

■ a *Make the curves rather flat.*

■ b *Make the combinations* k-r *and* r-k *somewhat shorter than the combined length of* r *and* k *when written by themselves.*

■ c *Make the combinations* gay-l *somewhat shorter than the combined length of* gay *and* l *when written by themselves.*

practice drill

Cream, crate, maker, mark, dark.
Gleam, glean, glare, legal.

224 Recall Chart

This chart contains all the brief forms in Chapter 4 and an illustration of many of the shorthand devices you studied in Chapters 1 through 4.

The chart contains 90 outlines. Can you read the entire chart in 7 minutes or less?

BRIEF FORMS

1	C	∪	𝓎	⁊	⌒	ℰ
2	)	⌒	)	₀	⌐	)
3	(	⌒	∠	⌐	⌒	∪

PHRASES

WORDS

Building Transcription Skills

225
Business
Vocabulary
Builder

commercials Advertisements broadcast on radio or television.

rejects Refuses to accept.

derive Receive.

sponsor One who pays the cost of a radio or television program in return for limited advertising time.

● Reading and Writing Practice

226   **Safe Driving**

any·one ②

fas·ten ③

④

5. Do you always ⑥

ar·ea ⑦

⑧

de·fen·sive·ly ⑨

ap·proaches ⑩

[198]

227 Advertising

wheth·er

com·mer·cials

lis·tens

ads

per·suade

Who Pays for Advertising?

buys

Truth in Advertising.

of·ten

praise

its

spon·sor

bor·ing

[404]

Secretarial Jobs
A Wide Range

Today's secretary can choose a job from many different fields. The positions range from those of a general secretarial nature to the highly specialized jobs in the legal, medical, or technical professions. The secretary's job options span a variety of private businesses and numerous public service fields. Positions are available in all geographical areas of the United States and in many other countries as well.

There are many fine opportunities for secretaries who are interested in developing their skills and increasing their knowledge in special areas. Let's take a look at just three of the many fascinating fields in which a secretary can become an active and indispensable participant.

Advertising and Public Relations

In the closely related fields of advertising and public relations, qualified secretaries are offered many challenging opportunities. In either field, the secretary must not only be able to work well under pressure but must also be able to communicate well with other people. The secretary must be people-oriented because employers in these fields deal constantly with clients, editors, account executives, freelance writers, artists, photographers, models, actors, and printers. The secretary must be able to work with details and be able to synchronize countless dates, facts, figures, faces, names, and sources. In addition, the secretary must be able to both organize and follow through on many complicated, long-range campaigns and projects.

Creativity is contagious, and the secretary in advertising and public relations has an enviable opportunity to cultivate special talents.

Government Service

The range of opportunities for the secretary in government is very wide. A civil service job may take the secretary to Washington, D.C. or to a number of other cities in the United States and other countries. The secretary may work for a senator, a representative, or a member of the President's staff. Or a position may be available with the Bureau of Indian Affairs, the Department of Housing and Urban Development, the Federal Bureau of Investigation, or with any number of other fascinating departments or agencies. The list is almost endless—and so is the challenge.

The Legal Field

The legal secretary may work for one attorney, for a large law firm, or for a corporation. The position may involve all types of legal work, or it may involve only one area, such as criminal, tax, or corporate law. The job may involve working for a judge whose court work is on the city, state, or national level. Regardless of the type of law office, the secretary must understand thoroughly the legal terminology and must be extremely accurate in all communication. The secretary may serve as receptionist, make appointments for clients, and notarize papers. Many times the job involves considerable responsibility in management of the business portion of the law practice. Of particular importance in every situation is the ability to keep close control of the employer's court calendar and the vital dates connected with each client's legal proceedings.

This is only a sampling of three of the many fields in which a secretary may work. Choose an area that matches your interests, and you are well on your way to an interesting, rewarding job in a secretarial field that fits you personally.

Principles

228 Brief Forms

difficult   ⟋⟍   success   ⟋⟍   request   ⟍₉

envelope   ⟍   satisfy,   ⟋   wish   ⟍
                       satisfactory

progress   ⟍   state   ⟍   under*   ⌒

*The outline for *under* is written above the following shorthand character. It is also used as a prefix form, as in:

underneath   ⌒₆   understudy   ⌒   undertake   ⌒

229 Cities and States

In your work as a stenographer and secretary, you will frequently have occasion to write geographical expressions. Here are a few important cities and states.

Cities

New York   ⟋⟍   Boston   ⟋   Los Angeles   ⟍₉

Chicago   ⟋   Philadelphia   ⟋   St. Louis   ⟋₃

States

Michigan   ⟋   Massachusetts   ⟍ℓ   Missouri   ⟍

Illinois   ℯ   Pennsylvania   6   California   ⟍ℯ

230 **Useful Business Phrases**

The following phrases are used so frequently in business that special forms have been provided for them. Study these phrases as you would study brief forms.

as soon as   ⟨shorthand⟩   *of course*   ⟨shorthand⟩   *let us*   ⟨shorthand⟩

as soon as possible   ⟨shorthand⟩   *to do*   ⟨shorthand⟩   *I hope*   ⟨shorthand⟩

Building Transcription Skills

231
Business Vocabulary Builder

competitors Rivals.
reverse *(adjective)* Opposite.
invaluable Priceless.

● Reading and Writing Practice

232 **Brief-Form Letter**

ap·proach·ing

sat·is·fy·ing

com·pet·i·tors

[144]

233

ap·pre·ci·ate

cus·tom·ers

co·op·er·a·tion

war·ran·ty [173]

234

ad·van·tage

be·lieve

con·fi·dent

im·me·di·ate·ly

[153]

235

code

re·li·able

[138]

236

reg·is·tered

[118]

Principles

237 Long ī and a Following Vowel

Any vowel following long ī is represented by a small circle within a large circle.

Compare: signs *science*

Spell: s-īah-n-s, science

trial   drier   appliance

client   prior   reliance

238 Word Beginnings En-, Un-

The word beginnings *en-, un-* are represented by *n.*

En-

Spell: en-j-oi, enjoy

enjoy   encounter   enrich

endeavor   engineering   encourage

Un-

Spell: un-p-a-d, unpaid

unpaid   unless   unfair

unpleasant   unsatisfactory   unfilled

239 In-, En-, Un- Followed by a Vowel

When *in-*, *en-*, or *un-* is followed by a vowel, the word beginning is written in full.

innovation *(outline)*   enact *(outline)*   unable *(outline)*

240 Useful Business Phrases

Here are additional frequently used phrases for which special forms have been provided. Study them as you would study brief forms.

more than *(outline)*   to us *(outline)*   your order *(outline)*

we hope *(outline)*   let me *(outline)*   you ordered *(outline)*

Building Transcription Skills

241
Business Vocabulary Builder

office appliances Calculators, typewriters, duplicators, etc.

laymen Persons who are not expert in a particular field.

unbiased Fair.

precision Exactness.

● Reading and Writing Practice

242 Brief-Form Review Letter

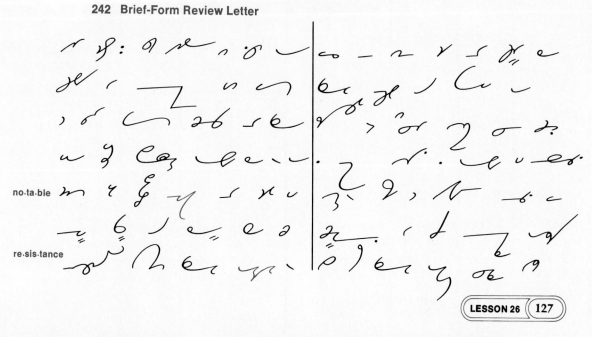

no·ta·ble

re·sis·tance

co·op·er·a·tion

ab [155]

243

com·plete·ly .

too

lay·men

un·bi·ased

cou·pon

[163]

244

un·pleas·ant

ac·knowl·edg·ment

pre·cious

[137]

245

en·gi·neer·ing

col·or

urge

proud

pre·ci·sion

view·ing

[140]

PROPORTION The writer who can read his shorthand notes fluently is the one who is careful of his
CHECKLIST proportions. In your shorthand writing, do you:

- 1 Make the large *a* circle huge; the small *e* circle tiny?
- 2 Make the straight strokes very straight and the curves very deep?
- 3 Make the *o* and *oo* hooks deep and narrow?
- 4 Make short strokes, such as *t* and *n*, very short and long strokes, such as *ted* and *men*, very long?

Principles

246 Brief Forms

After you have learned the following group of nine brief forms, you will have only two more groups to go!

particular	speak	regard
probable	idea	newspaper
regular	subject	opinion

247 Ng

The sound of *ng,* as in *sing,* is written ‿ .

Compare: seen ⟂ sing ⟂

Spell: *s-e-ing, sing*

sing	long	bring
sang	spring	single
song	strong	young

248 Ngk

The sound of *ngk,* as in *sink,* is written ‿ .

Compare: seem ⟂ sink ⟂

Spell: *s-e-ink, sink; oo-ink-l, uncle*

rank	bank	anxious

frank		banquet		uncle	
ink		link		blank	

249 Omission of Vowel Preceding -tion

When *t, d, n,* or *m* is followed by *-ition, -ation,* the circle is omitted.

edition		reputation		donation	
addition		invitation		station	
condition		permission		stationed	

Building Transcription Skills

250 Business Vocabulary Builder

enlightening Instructional.

medium A means of conveying information.

automation The state of being operated automatically.

● Reading and Writing Practice

251 Brief-Form Letter

ac·cept·ed

pi·o·neer

au·di·ence

101-5151

[163]

[154]

252

edi·tions . 24

253

its

7   15

5   Des Moines

po·ten·tial

qual·i·fied

pro·gres·sive

hon·ored

[171] (350/)

255

254

new·ly
mar·ried

pre·mi·um

ques·tion·naire

[130]

May·or

pre·vails

mi·nor

ma·jor

[111]

Principles

256 Ah, Aw

A dot is used for *a* in words beginning *ah* and *aw*.

   Spell: a-h-e-d, ahead; a-oo-a, away

ahead .ᵈ   await .ᵧ   aware .ᵣ

away .ᵈ   awake .ᵧ   award .ᵤ

257 X

The letter x is usually represented by an *s* written with a slight backward slant.

   Compare: miss ___ₑ   mix ___ₑ

         fees ᵈ   *fix* ᵈ

   Spell: m-e-x, mix

box ᵘ   tax ℓ   fix ᵈ

index ℓ   taxes ℓ   fixes ᵈ

258 Omission of Short U

In the body of a word the sound of short *u*, as in *done*, is omitted:

   Before N

done ╱   luncheon ⌐ᶻ   begun ᵘ

fun ᒎ   run ⌣   refund ᵧ

Before M

sum		come		welcome		
summer		become		lumber		

Before a Straight Downstroke

rush		touch		judge		
such		much		budget		

Building Transcription Skills

259	**peruse** Examine; study.
Business	**budget** The amount of money set aside for a particular purpose.
Vocabulary	**talents** Abilities.
Builder	

● Reading and Writing Practice

260 Brief-Form Review Letter

your

han·dling

suf·fered

[151]

261

touch

pe·ruse

an·swer

[145]

262

bud·get

their

al·ways

48

wel·come [151]

263

re·ceipt

suc·cess

ap·pli·cants

[104]

264

de·ci·sions

sim·ply

[99]

Principles

265 Brief Forms

You have only one more group to learn after this one.

responsible	publish, publication	usual
worth	ordinary	world
public	experience	recognize

266 Word Beginning Ex-

The word beginning *ex-* is represented by *e-s.*

Spell: ex-p-n-sez, expenses

expenses	extremely	extent
expert	exactly	expiration
expectation	exceeded	extra

267 Word Ending -ful

The word ending *-ful* is represented by *f.*

Spell: k-a-r-ful, careful

careful	useful	helpful
delightful	successful	helpfully
thoughtful	doubtful	helpfulness

268 Word Endings -cal, -cle

Word endings *-cal* and *-cle* (and the preceding vowel) are represented by a disjoined *k*.

Spell: t-e-k-n-ical, technical; a-r-t-ical, article

technical	practical	articles
medical	typical	physical
logical	economical	physically

Building Transcription Skills

269
SIMILAR-WORDS
DRILL
it's, its

it's Contraction for *it is.*

It's his day to wash the dishes.

its Possessive form of *it.*

Its operating efficiency makes cooking on our stove a delight.

270
Business
Vocabulary
Builder

maximum The most.

exceeded Went beyond.

franchises Rights granted to market a company's goods in a particular territory.

● Reading and Writing Practice

271 Brief-Form Letter

it's

state's

ex·pe·ri·enced

mon·ey's

its

272

per·son·nel

[140]

an·a·lyzes

their

10

cop·ies

[183]

273

en·joy·able

au·di·ence

com·plete·ly

speak·er's

[198]

274

own·ing

fran·chises

quite

ev·ery day

[147]

RECALL

After studying the new shorthand devices in Lessons 25 through 29, you have earned another breathing spell! Therefore, you will find no new shorthand strokes or principles in Lesson 30.

In this lesson you will find an Accuracy Practice devoted to the curved strokes of Gregg Shorthand, a Recall Chart, and a Reading and Writing Practice that offers you some interesting suggestions on how to be a good conversationalist.

Accuracy Practice

To get the most benefit from this Accuracy Practice, be sure to follow the procedures suggested on page 115.

275   **B**   **V**   **P**   **F**   **S**

To write these strokes accurately:

- a *Give them approximately the slant indicated by the dotted lines.*
- b *Make the curve deep at the beginning of v, f, comma s; make the curve deep at the end of b, p, left s.*

practice drill

Puts, spare, business, bears, stairs, sphere, leaves, briefs.

276 **P-r** **P-l** **B-r** **B-l**

To write these combinations accurately:

- a *Write each without a pause between the first and second letter of each combination.*
- b *Watch your proportions carefully.*

practice drill

Press, pray, prim, plan, plate, place.
Brim, bridge, bread, blame, blast.

277 **F-r** **F-l**

To write these combinations accurately:

- *Write them with one sweep of the pen, with no stop between the f and the r or l.*

practice drill

Free, freeze, frame, flee, flame, flap.

278 Recall Chart

The following chart contains brief forms, phrasing principles, and word-building principles you studied in Chapter 5.

Can you read the entire chart in 6 minutes or less?

BRIEF FORMS AND DERIVATIVES

PHRASES

WORDS

Building Transcription Skills

279
Business
Vocabulary
Builder

pastimes Things that amuse.

decipher To make out the meaning of.

facial Of or relating to the face.

● Reading and Writing Practice

Reading Scoreboard If you have been studying each Reading and Writing Practice faithfully, your reading speed has no doubt increased since you last measured it in Lesson 18. Let us measure that increase on the first reading of the material in Lesson 30. The following table will help you:

Lesson 30 contains 715 words

If you read Lesson 30 in 20 minutes your reading rate is 36 words a minute
If you read Lesson 30 in 23 minutes your reading rate is 31 words a minute
If you read Lesson 30 in 26 minutes your reading rate is 28 words a minute
If you read Lesson 30 in 29 minutes your reading rate is 25 words a minute
If you read Lesson 30 in 31 minutes your reading rate is 23 words a minute
If you read Lesson 30 in 34 minutes your reading rate is 21 words a minute

---

If you can read Lesson 30 in 20 minutes or less, you are doing well. If you take considerably longer than 34 minutes, perhaps you should review your homework procedures. For example, are you:

■ 1 Practicing in a quiet place at home?

■ 2 Practicing without the radio or television set on?

■ 3 Spelling aloud any words that you cannot read immediately?

280 The Value of Exercise

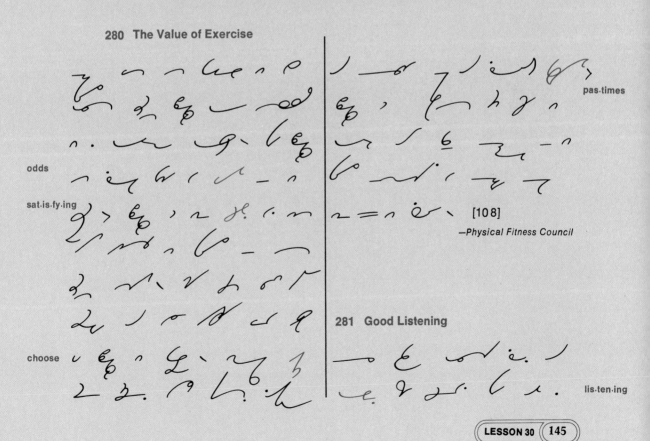

pas·times

odds

sat·is·fy·ing

[108]
—*Physical Fitness Council*

281 Good Listening

choose

lis·ten·ing

de·pen·dent

of·ten

de·ci·pher

some·times

fa·cial

Listening in Business.

ar·eas

ex·pe·ri·enced

rec·og·nize

au·di·ence

Good Listening

rep·re·sen·ta·tive

re·spon·si·bly

duties

We All Listen a Lot.

than

sur·vey

stud·ies

Listening on the Job.

tan·gi·ble

crit·i·cism

[607]

The Secretary Communicates

Taking dictation, writing letters, answering the telephone, greeting visitors, interacting with co-workers or clients—all are part of the secretary's job and all depend on the ability to communicate.

In the office, *communications* refers to anything having to do with the written or spoken word. Therefore, most of what the secretary does in the office involves communicating.

Written communications are a vital part of any business. It is the secretary who is responsible for preparing most, if not all, of such communications. An effective business letter, for example, promotes goodwill and elicits the reader's favorable reaction toward both the writer and the organization represented. In all correspondence, the secretary is responsible for accuracy, appearance, and completeness. This means that no less than perfect grammar, spelling, punctuation, and typing will do. It also means that all facts and figures, including addresses and dates, must be accurate.

To produce superior correspondence, the secretary should have a thorough knowledge of English. Grammatical errors may not always be noticed during dictation, but they show up immediately on a typed page. The secretary must learn to correct such errors before they reach the printed page. There is little value in typing at top speed if the resulting work must be redone because of misspelled words.

Employers expect their secretaries to spell correctly words which are in general use and to learn to spell technical words that are part of the language of the particular business or profession. Punctuation, too, must be correct. If punctuation does not clarify the writing, the reader may misinterpret the ideas. Incorrect punctuation can easily lead to misunderstanding.

Other important ways of communicating are speaking and listening. The good secretary can handle visitors and telephone callers intelligently and courteously by speaking in a well-modulated voice, enunciating distinctly, choosing words that convey thoughts clearly, and expressing sincere interest.

Studies have shown that executives may spend one-half to two-thirds of their time listening to others. Secretaries must listen nearly as much. Misunderstandings are avoided and work production is increased when the secretary listens intelligently.

Writing, speaking, and listening are skills every secretary needs in order to fulfill one of the most important aspects of the secretarial job—communication.

LESSON 31

Principles

282 Brief Forms

This is the last group of brief forms you will have to learn.

never	throughout	govern
quantity	object	correspond, correspondence
executive	character	

283 Word Ending -ure

The word ending -ure is represented by r.

Spell: f-u-t-r, future

future	venture	nature
picture	miniature	natural

284 Word Ending -ual

The word ending -ual is represented by l.

Spell: gay-r-a-d-l, gradual

gradual	individual	annual
eventually	actual	equal

Building Transcription Skills

285
PUNCTUATION
PRACTICE

Another skill you must possess if you are to be a successful stenographer or secretary is the ability to punctuate correctly. Some executives dictate punctuation, but most of them rely on their stenographers or secretaries to supply the proper punctuation when they transcribe.

To sharpen your punctuation skill, you will hereafter give special attention to punctuation in each Reading and Writing Practice. In the lessons ahead you will review nine of the most common uses of the comma. Each time one of these uses of the comma occurs in the Reading and Writing Practice, it will be encircled in the shorthand, thus forcefully calling it to your attention.

Practice
Suggestions

If you follow these suggestions in your homework practice hereafter, your ability to punctuate should improve noticeably.

■ 1 Read carefully the explanation of each comma usage (for example, the explanation of the parenthetical comma given below) to be sure that you understand it. You will encounter many illustrations of each comma usage in the Reading and Writing Practice exercises, so that eventually you will acquire the knack of applying it correctly.

■ 2 Continue to read and copy each Reading and Writing Practice as you have done before. However, add these two important steps:

■ a Each time you see an encircled comma in the Reading and Writing Practice, note the reason for its use, which is indicated directly above the encircled comma.

■ b As you copy the Reading and Writing Practice in your shorthand notebook, insert the commas in your shorthand notes, encircling them as in the textbook.

PUNCTUATION
PRACTICE
, parenthetical

A word or a phrase that is used parenthetically (that is, one not necessary to the grammatical completeness of the sentence) should be set off by commas.

If the parenthetical expression occurs at the end of the sentence, only one comma is used.

There is, of course, *no charge for our services.*

Please let us know, Mr. Strong, *if we can help you.*

We actually print your picture on the card, Ms. Green.

Each time a parenthetical expression occurs in the Reading and Writing Practice, it will be indicated thus in the shorthand: ^{par}

286
Business
Vocabulary
Builder

miniature A copy which has been reduced in size.

ventures Business matters involving risk.

exhausted Used up.

Reading and Writing Practice

287 Brief-Form Letter

gov·ern·ment

cor·re·spon·dence

sym·pa·thy

sta·tio·nery

crit·i·cal·ly

[178]

288

ap·ply·ing

amazed

– 1978

re·spon·si·ble

ex·cel·lence

par

par

bright

rec·om·mend

par

[167]

[173]

289

its

290

Phil·a·del·phia

1785

Man·u·al

par

opin·ion

pri·ma·ry

suc·cess·ful

par

par

cop·ies

ac·knowl·edge

par

[131]

291

ac·cept

par

par

[101]

292

par man·u·al

com·pli·ments

par

suc·cess

[102]

Principles

293 Word Ending -ily

The word ending *-ily* is represented by a narrow loop.

    Compare: ready   readily

    Spell: r-e-d-ily, readily

easily	speedily	family
steadily	temporarily	families

▶ Note the special joining of *s* used in *families*. The special joining enables us to form an outline that is easily read.

294 Word Beginning Al-

The word beginning *al-* is expressed by o.

    Spell: all-m-o-s-t, almost

almost	altogether	although
also	already	alter

295 Word Beginnings Dis-, Des-

The word beginnings *dis-*, *des-* are represented by *d-s*.

    Spell: dis-k-oo-s, discuss; dis-k-r-ī-b, describe

Dis-

discuss   *(shorthand)*   disturb   *(shorthand)*   disposal   *(shorthand)*

discussion   *(shorthand)*   discover   *(shorthand)*   discourage   *(shorthand)*

Des-

describe   *(shorthand)*   destination   *(shorthand)*   destroy   *(shorthand)*

Building Transcription Skills

296
PUNCTUATION
PRACTICE
, apposition

An expression in apposition (that is, a word or a phrase or a clause that identifies or explains other terms) should be set off by commas. When an expression in apposition occurs at the end of a sentence, only one comma is necessary.

My employer, Mr. Frank Smith, *is on a business trip.*

I will see him on Friday, June 15, *at 3 o'clock.*

His book, Principles of Accounting, *is out of stock.*

For more information call Mr. Brown, *our production manager.*

▶ Note: When the clarifying term is very closely connected with the principal noun so that the sense would not be complete without the added term, no commas are required.

My brother Fred *arrived yesterday.*

The word embarrassed *is often misspelled.*

Each time an expression in apposition occurs in the Reading and Writing Practice, it will be indicated thus in the shorthand: $\overset{ap}{\underset{\smile}{\cdot}}$

297
Business
Vocabulary
Builder

fumes Irritating smoke or gas.

sturdily Strongly; substantially.

apathy Lack of interest or concern; indifference.

endorsement Approval.

● Reading and Writing Practice

298 Brief-Form Review Letter

or·ga·ni·za·tion

(shorthand outlines)

pol·lu·tion

ap

stur·di·ly

de·stroy
al·ter

than

cor·re·spon·dence   ap

de·scrip·tive   par

ap

de·scribes

ad·van·tages
par

al·ready

[162]

[158]

299   300

303

[shorthand outlines]

re·ceived par

ap

15

dis·turb·ing

ap

in·ject

[116]

[87]

DICTATION CHECKLIST

When you take dictation, do you—

■ 1 Make every effort to keep up with the dictator?

■ 2 Refer to your textbook whenever you are in doubt about the outline for a word or phrase?

■ 3 Insert periods and question marks in your shorthand notes?

■ 4 Make a real effort to observe good proportion as you write—making large circles large, small circles small, etc.?

■ 5 Do you write down the first column of your notebook and then down the second column?

Principles

304 Word Beginnings For-, Fore-

The word beginnings *for-, fore-* are represented by *f*.

Spell: *for-gay-e-v, forgive*

forgive	inform	foreclose
forget	information	afford
form	force	comfortable

The *f* is joined with an angle to *r* or *l* to indicate that it represents a word beginning. The *f* is disjoined if the following character is a vowel.

forerunner	forlorn	forever

305 Word Beginning Fur-

The word beginning *fur-* is also represented by *f*.

Spell: *fur-n-a-s, furnace*

furnace	furthermore	refurnish
further	furnish	furniture

306 Ago in Phrases

In expressions of time, *ago* is represented by *gay*.

weeks ago	several days ago	months ago
years ago	long time ago	minutes ago

Building Transcription Skills

307
PUNCTUATION
PRACTICE
, series

When the last member of a series of three or more items is preceded by *and* or *or*, place a comma before the conjunction as well as between the other items.

For his birthday he received a tie, a shirt, and a wallet.

I need a person to take dictation, to answer the phone, and to greet callers.

I can see her on July 18, on July 19, or on July 30.

▶ Note: Some authorities prefer to omit the comma before the conjunction. In your shorthand textbooks, however, the comma will always be inserted before the conjunction.

Each time a series occurs in the Reading and Writing Practice, it will be indicated thus in the shorthand: ser

308
Business
Vocabulary
Builder

suites *(of furniture)* Sets of matched furniture for a room.

refurnish To equip with new furniture.

canceled check A check which has been processed by a bank.

● Reading and Writing Practice

309 **Brief-Form Review Letter**

par

ef·fect
suites

re·fur·nish

[133]

char·ac·ter

ser

310

show·room

cor·re·spon·dence

ser

re·spon·si·ble

ser

fur·ther·more

par

ours

[166]

311

ap

15

ap

Fac·to·ry

can·celed

is·sues

ser

par

re·ceipt

[119]

312

ap

For·ty

ap

rec·og·nized

con·quered

prac·ti·cal   ser

com·pa·nies

par

cre·ate   ser

Feb·ru·ary

suite

314

[104]

[124]

313

re·cent·ly

ap

over·coat   ser

[50]

Principles

315 Want in Phrases

In phrases, *want* is represented by the *nt* blend.

you want   ∿   I wanted   ⌀   do you want   ⟋

if you want   ⟑   we want   ⟋   he wants   ⟍

316 Ort

The *r* is omitted in the combination *ort.*

Spell: re-p-o-t, report

report   ⟋   airport   ⟋   quarterly   ⟋

support   ⟍   export   ⟍   mortal   ⟋

317 R Omitted in -ern, -erm

The *r* is omitted in the combinations *tern, term, thern, therm, dern.*

Spell: t-e-n, turn

turn   ⟋   term   ⟋   southern   ⟋

return   ⟋   termination   ⟋   thermometer   ⟋

eastern   ⟋   determine   ⟋   modern   ⟋

318 Md, Mt

By rounding off the angle between *m-d,* we obtain the fluent *md* blend. The same stroke also represents *mt.*

Md, Mt   ⟋

Compare: seem ⟍ *seemed* ⟍

Spell: s-e-emd, seemed; emt-e, empty

named	↗	informed	↗	termed	↗
framed	↗	confirmed	↗	empty	↗
claimed	↗	welcomed	↗	prompt	↗

Building Transcription Skills

319
SIMILAR-WORDS
DRILL
addition, edition

addition Anything added.

[shorthand outline]

This picture is a fine addition to our collection.

edition All the copies of a book published at one time.

[shorthand outline] 50,

We sold 50,000 copies of the second edition of the book.

320
Business
Vocabulary
Builder

undependable Unreliable.

quarterly Every three months.

confirmed Acknowledged.

● Reading and Writing Practice

321 **Brief-Form Review Letter**

par
var·ied

un·de·pend·able

edi·tion

ap

re·spon·si·ble *(par)*

ad·di·tion

ad·ver·tis·ing *(ap)*

[178]

322

(par)

fam·i·ly

year's

(ap)

ser **Jan·u·ary**

mod·ern

Phil·a·del·phia

[196]

323

dif·fer·ence

ser 10,

ser

wor·ry

eco·nom·i·cal

dis·tance

ser

[135]

324

re·ceived

passed

ap

10

5

[Shorthand reading passages 324 and 325]

ac·cept

par

[110]

325

ex·pe·ri·enc·ing

ser

par Mas·sa·chu·setts

ar [82]

Principles

326 Word Beginnings Inter-, Intr-, Enter-, Entr-

The similar sounding word beginnings *inter-, intr-, enter-, entr-* (and the word *enter*) are represented by a disjoined *n*. This disjoined word beginning, as well as other disjoined word beginnings that you will study in later lessons, is placed above the line of writing close to the remainder of the word.

Inter-

Spell: inter-s-t, interest

interest	international	interfere
interview	interrupted	interval

Intr-

Spell: intro-d-oo-s, introduce

introduce	introduced	introduction

Enter-, Entr-

Spell: enter-ing, entering

entering	enterprises	entrance
entered	entertain	entrances

327 Word Ending -ings

The word ending *-ings* is represented by a disjoined left *s*.

Spell: o-p-n-ings, openings

openings	meetings	earnings
evenings	dealings	proceedings

328 Omission of Words in Phrases

It is often possible to omit one or more unimportant words in a shorthand phrase to gain writing speed. In the phrase *one of the*, for example, the word *of* is omitted; we write *one the*. When transcribing, the stenographer will insert *of*, as the phrase would make no sense without that word.

one of the ∿	some of them ∿	many of these ——↶
one of these ∿	men and women ——↷	up to date ↺
one or two ∿	in the world ⌒	in the future ⌲

Building Transcription Skills

329
Business
Vocabulary
Builder

turnover The number of persons hired within a period to replace those leaving a work force.

perplexing Puzzling.

eligible Qualified.

limousine A large chauffeur-driven sedan.

● Reading and Writing Practice

330 Brief-Form and Phrase Letter

This letter contains many brief forms and derivatives as well as several illustrations of the phrasing principle you studied in this lesson.

dis·turbed

par
aware
ex·pense
lose

el·i·gi·ble

suc·cess·ful·ly

crit·i·cal

85,

par

[187]

331

morn·ing's

par

ap

sym·pa·thies

ap

332

ser

prin·ci·ples

[148]

crews

ap

ser

un·in·ter·rupt·ed

bored

prob·a·bly

par

lim·ou·sine

cit·ies

par

(118–116½)

[172]

[154]

333

334

ac·knowl·edg·ment

ap

au·di·ence

par

① ② 15 ③

18

[108]

ac·cept

RECALL

Lesson 36 is another breather. In Lesson 36 you will find the last principle of joining, a chart that contains a review of shorthand devices you studied in Lessons 1 through 35, and a Reading and Writing Practice that you should find interesting and informative.

Principles of Joining

335 The word endings *-ure* and *-ual* are represented by *r* and *l* except when those endings are preceded by a downstroke.

nature	procedure	creature
equal	gradual	annual

but

pressure	treasure	insured
casual	visual	visually

Accuracy Practice

336   **O**   **On**   **Sho**   **Non**

To write these combinations accurately:

■ a *Keep the* o *hook narrow, being sure that the* beginning *and* end *are on the same level of writing, as indicated by the dotted line.*

- **b** *Keep the o in on and sho parallel with the consonant, as indicated by the dotted line.*
- **c** *Make the beginning of the o in non retrace end of the first n*
- **d** *Avoid a point at the curved parts indicated by the arrows.*

practice drill

Of, know, low, own, home, hot, known, moan, shown.

337   **OO**   **Noo**   **Noom**

To write these combinations accurately:
- **a** *Keep the oo hook narrow and deep.*
- **b** *Keep the beginning and end of the hook on the same level of writing.*
- **c** *In noo and noom, keep the hook parallel with the straight line that precedes it.*
- **d** *In noom, retrace the beginning of the m on the bottom of the oo hook.*
- **e** *Avoid a point at the places indicated by arrows.*

practice drill

You-your, yours truly, you would, to, do, noon, moon, renewal.

338   **Hard**   **Hailed**

To write these combinations accurately:
- **a** *Give the end of the r and of the l a lift upward.*
- **b** *Do not lift the end too soon, or the strokes may resemble the nd, md combinations.*

practice drill

Neared, feared, cheered, dared, hold, sold, bold.

339 **Recall Chart**

This chart contains illustrations of shorthand principles you studied in previous lessons. There are 12 brief forms and derivatives, 12 phrases, and 66 words in the chart.

Can you read the entire chart in 5 minutes?

BRIEF FORMS AND DERIVATIVES

PHRASES

WORDS

Building Transcription Skills

340
Business Vocabulary Builder

effecting Bringing about; resulting in.

capacity Ability.

accord (*verb*) Give to.

● Reading and Writing Practice

341 The Secretary in Business

ef·fect·ing

ar·eas

The secretary and

Secretarial Positions Differ.

af·fect·ed

or·ga·ni·za·tion
ser

en·ter·prise

pri·mar·i·ly

[486]

342 Courtesy and Success

calm

odd

iden·ti·cal

co·op·er·a·tion   ser

Our courtesy

ser

an·swer

con·scious

[216]

343 Sleep and Diet

ser

snack

weight

ser

cal·o·ries

[113]

The Secretary Takes Dictation

The ability to take dictation is the core of the secretary's job, but just being able to write shorthand is not enough. Success in this important part of the secretary's work will depend upon writing good, sensible notes which can be transcribed easily and quickly with accuracy.

Handling dictation may be the secretary's most important task. The secretary must be ready to take dictation whenever the employer wants to give it. When the boss is ready to dictate, all other work must be put aside.

Many secretaries form the good habit of checking—the first thing in the morning—to be sure that their dictation tools are in order. "I wouldn't think of answering my employer's call without a shorthand notebook and my pen," says one secretary. When summoned to the boss's office, the secretary is ready to answer promptly with an open shorthand notebook and a pen.

During the dictation session, the secretary makes it possible for the employer to get the work done as expeditiously as possible. All dictation and instructions are recorded accurately. Nothing is done to divert or annoy the dictator.

The dictating habits of employers vary greatly. For some, dictating is hard work and ideas come slowly. Some employers may pause for long periods during a difficult letter or report, but once they clarify the idea they want to express, they are likely to reel it off very rapidly. Other employers, more gifted at expressing themselves, dictate at a fairly regular or brisk pace.

Employers expect their secretaries to be proficient shorthand writers, able to keep up with the dictation no matter how fast the pace becomes. True, if the dictation speed of an entire letter is average, it may seem fairly slow; yet during every dictation period there are many times when a high shorthand speed is required to keep up.

To maintain your shorthand skill, use it outside the office too. Try using it for all personal notes and instructions. Create opportunities to practice reading and writing shorthand whenever you can. Following a dictation session, the secretary should get all the instructions and clarifications needed before leaving the boss's office so that it will not be necessary to interrupt later. All instructions should be written so that there is no need to rely on memory alone. Much of the business conducted today takes the form of letters and other written communications. To expedite communicating information, today's secretary must be able to take and transcribe dictation both quickly and accurately.

Principles

344 Word Ending -ingly

The word ending *-ingly* is represented by a disjoined *e* circle.

Spell: in-k-r-e-s-ingly, increasingly

increasingly	convincingly	willingly
exceedingly	amazingly	interestingly

345 Word Beginning Im-

The word beginning *im-* is represented by *m*.

Spell: im-p-r-e-s, impress

impress	impartial	import
impressive	improvement	impact

346 Word Beginning Em-

The word beginning *em-* is also represented by *m*.

Spell: em-p-ī-r, empire

empire	emphatically	employee
embarrass	embraced	employer

347 Im-, Em- Followed by a Vowel

When *im-*, *em-* are followed by a vowel, they are written in full.

immodest   immoral   emotional

348 Omission of Minor Vowel

When two vowel sounds come together, the minor vowel may be omitted.

various		period		situate	
serious		genuine		situated	
previous		theory		situation	

Building Transcription Skills

349
PUNCTUATION
PRACTICE
, if clause

A subordinate (or introductory) clause followed by a main clause is separated from the main clause by a comma. A subordinate clause is often introduced by subordinating conjunctions including *if, as, when, though, although, because,* and others. In this lesson you will consider only subordinate clauses introduced by *if.*

If you complete the work before 5 o'clock, *you may leave.*

If I cannot come, *I will call you.*

If John is ill, *he should stay home.*

Each time a subordinate clause beginning with *if* occurs in the Reading and Writing Practice, it will be indicated thus in the shorthand: ^{if}

350
Business
Vocabulary
Builder

impartially Fairly.

emphatically Forcefully.

reimbursed Paid back.

● Reading and Writing Practice

351 Brief-Form Review Letter

un·usu·al

par (with shorthand symbol)

ser (with shorthand symbol)

pe·ri·od·i·cals

re·quest

if

[181]

352

the·o·ries

ser

par (with shorthand symbol)

re·im·bursed

[146]

353

if

ap

16

25

em·ploy·ee

el·i·gi·ble

25=

im·pres·sive

ser

won

ser

par

ser

25 =

ap

15

pre·vi·ous

if

par

sat·is·fac·to·ry

[170]

354

if

①

the·o·ries

ser

ser

②

③

ser

im·par·tial·ly

④

⑤

amaz·ing·ly

if

par

[157]

LESSON 38

Principles

355 **Word Ending -ship**

The word ending -*ship* is represented by a disjoined *ish*.

Spell: s-t-e-m-ship, steamship

steamship	membership	fellowship
friendship	relationships	leadership

356 **Word Beginning Sub-**

The word beginning *sub-* is represented by *s*.

Spell: sub-m-e-t, submit

submit	subscription	substantial
subscribe	subdivision	suburban

357 **Word Ending -ulate**

The word ending -*ulate* is represented by a disjoined *oo* hook.

Spell: r-e-gay-ulate, regulate

regulate	congratulate	tabulator
stimulate	formulate	calculated

358 Word Ending -ulation

The word ending -ulation is represented by *oo-shun*.

Spell: r-e-gay-ulation, regulation

regulation   accumulation   stimulation

insulation   circulation   congratulations

359 Word Ending -rity

The word ending -rity (and a preceding vowel) is represented by a disjoined *r*.

Spell: m-a-j-rity, majority

majority   prosperity   charity

security   sincerity   authority

Building Transcription Skills

360
PUNCTUATION PRACTICE
, as clause

A subordinate clause introduced by *as* and followed by a main clause is separated from the main clause by a comma.

As you know, *you have not yet paid your June bill.*

As I cannot attend the meeting, *I will send my assistant.*

Each time a subordinate clause beginning with *as* occurs in the Reading and Writing Practice, it will be indicated thus in the shorthand:

361
Business Vocabulary Builder

prosperity Economic well-being.

subsidiary A company owned by another.

proceeds *(noun)* Income.

● Reading and Writing Practice

362 Brief-Form Review Letter

ex·pe·ri·enced

ser

sub·stan·tial·ly

sub·sid·iary

Hous·ton

prob·a·bly

any·thing

an·swer

sub·scrip·tion

ar·ti·cles

363

[196]

[170]

364

char·i·ty

ap
,

pro·ceeds

29

50/

par
,

gen·er·os·i·ty

[118]

365

as
,

pleas·ant

[104]

Principles

366   Word Ending -lity

The word ending -*lity* (and a preceding vowel) is represented by a disjoined *l*.

> *Spell: a-b-lity, ability*

ability	$\mathcal{C}$	dependability		utility	
facility		locality		realities	
possibility		personality		qualities	

367   Word Ending -lty

The word ending *lty* (and a preceding vowel) is also represented by a disjoined *l*.

> *Spell: f-a-k-ulty, faculty*

faculty		penalty		royalty	

368   Word Ending -self

The word ending -*self* is represented by *s*.

> *Spell: h-e-r-self, herself; it-self, itself*

herself		himself		myself	
itself		yourself		oneself	

369   Word Ending -selves

The word ending -*selves* is represented by *ses*.

Spell: them-selves, themselves

themselves ⌐⌐ *ourselves* ↙ *yourselves* ↗

Building Transcription Skills

370
PUNCTUATION
PRACTICE
, when clause

A clause introduced by *when* and followed by the main clause is separated from the main clause by a comma.

When I was in Dallas, *I attended three meetings.*

When you do not pay your bills, *you are endangering your credit.*

Each time a subordinate clause beginning with *when* occurs in the Reading and Writing Practice, it will be indicated thus in the shorthand: when

371
Business
Vocabulary
Builder

individuality Total character distinguishing a person or thing from another.
stability Firmness.
integrity Honesty.

● Reading and Writing Practice

372   Brief-Form Review Letter

im·me·di·ate·ly

if

[161]

373

prac·ti·cal

ser

var·i·ous

par

20

ser

qual·i·ty

ar·ea

when

par

dis·cuss

[182]

374

cus·tom·er

ap

due

sub·stan·tial

prompt·ly

re·mit·tances

ap ,

par ,

par ,

if ,

[135]

375

route

gov·ern·ment

par ,

as ,

par·tic·u·lar·ly

text

when ,

be·lieve

as ,

pro·ceed

[150]

LESSON 40

Principles

376 Abbreviated Words—in Families

Many long words may be abbreviated in shorthand by dropping the endings. This device is, of course, used in longhand, as *Jan.* for *January*. The extent to which you can avail yourself of this device will depend on your familiarity with the words and with the subject matter of the dictation. Whenever you are in doubt as to whether you should abbreviate a word or write it out, write it out!

The ending of a word is not dropped when a special shorthand word-ending form has been provided, such as *-cal* in *practical*.

Notice how many of the words written with this abbreviating device fall naturally into families of similar endings.

-quent

frequent	consequent, consequence	subsequent
frequently	consequently	eloquent

-tribute

attribute	distribute	distribution
contribute	distributed	distributor

-quire

inquire	inquired	inquiry
require	required	requirement

-titute

substitute	institute	constitution

-titude

aptitude *(shorthand)*   gratitude *(shorthand)*   attitude *(shorthand)*

Building Transcription Skills

377
PUNCTUATION
PRACTICE
, introductory

A comma is used to separate a subordinate (or introductory) clause from a following main clause. You have already studied the application of this rule to subordinate clauses introduced by *if, as,* and *when.* Here are additional examples:

> While I understand the statement, *I do not agree with it.*

> Although it was only 3 o'clock, *he closed the office.*

> Before you sign the contract, *discuss it with your lawyer.*

A comma is also used after introductory words or phrases such as *furthermore,* on *the contrary,* and *for instance.*

> Furthermore, *the report was incomplete.*

> On the contrary, *you are the one who is responsible.*

> For your convenience in sending your check, *I am enclosing an envelope.*

Each time a subordinate word, phrase, or clause other than one beginning with *if, as,* or *when* occurs in the Reading and Writing Practice, it will be indicated thus in the shorthand: ^{intro} ⌣

▶ Note: If the subordinate clause or other introductory expression follows the main clause, the comma is usually not necessary.

> *I am enclosing an envelope for your convenience in sending your check.*

378
Business
Vocabulary
Builder

atlas A bound collection of maps.

maintenance The upkeep of property or equipment.

endeavor *(noun)* A serious, determined effort.

● Reading and Writing Practice

379 Brief-Form Review Letter

(shorthand outlines)

con·fer·ence   intro   intro

ex·cel·lent

ban·quet   ap

intro

in·quired

par

oc·ca·sion

intro

ar·ea

[176]

380

lease

when

ser   fu·el

intro

intro   ve·hi·cle

if

if

as   re·al·ize

[138]

381

re·ferred [shorthand outline]

as [shorthand outline]

intro [shorthand outline]

re·quests [shorthand outline]

readi·ly par [shorthand outline]

un·pleas·ant [shorthand outline]

par [shorthand outline]

en·deav·or [shorthand outline] [139]

382

[shorthand outlines] 20

ap [shorthand outline] 15 0

ur·gent [shorthand outline]

[shorthand outline] 20

intro [shorthand outline]

co·op·er·a·tion

sat·is·fied

par [shorthand outline] [138]

383

[shorthand outlines]

Man·u·al

ap

com·mer·cial

ap

col·ors

— 4

piece

intro

in·qui·ries

[132]

384

196 LESSON 40

wom·en

par

com·plete·ly

fur·ther·more

intro

ser

par

[135]

LESSON 41

Principles

385 Abbreviated Words—in Families (Continued)

-graph

phonograph ___   photograph ___   photographically ___

paragraph ___   photographic ___   autographed ___

telegraph ___   photographs ___   stenographer ___

386 Abbreviated Words—Not in Families

The ending may be omitted from long words even though they do not fall into a family.

anniversary ___   statistic ___   reluctant, reluctance ___

convenient, convenience ___   statistics ___   privilege ___

significant, significance ___   statistical ___   privileged ___

memorandum ___   equivalent ___   privileges ___

387 Word Beginning Trans-

The word beginning *trans-* is represented by a disjoined *t.*

Spell: trans-a-k-t, transact

transact ___   transmitted ___   transfer ___

transaction ___   translation ___   transcribe ___

transportation ___   transistor ___   transplant ___

Building Transcription Skills

388
SIMILAR-WORDS DRILL
assistance, assistants

assistance Help.

[shorthand outlines]

Thank you for the assistance you gave me with my term paper.

assistants Helpers.

[shorthand outlines]

One of my assistants will discuss the matter with you.

389
Business Vocabulary Builder

transmitted Forwarded; handed over.
reluctant Unwilling.
autographed Signed by hand.

● Reading and Writing Practice

390 Brief-Form Review Letter

[shorthand outlines with marginal notes: par, when, grat·i·tude, intro, as·sis·tance, and Gov·er·nor]

per·son·al [shorthand] [129]

391

an·ni·ver·sa·ry [shorthand]

intro [symbol]

priv·i·lege [shorthand]

par [symbol]

wouldn't [shorthand]

intro [symbol]

if [symbol] [shorthand] ser [symbol]

en·ve·lope [shorthand] [173]

392 [shorthand]

ap [symbol]

oc·ca·sion [shorthand]

as [symbol]

max·i·mum [shorthand]

25' [shorthand] 150/ max·i·mum

[shorthand] 250/

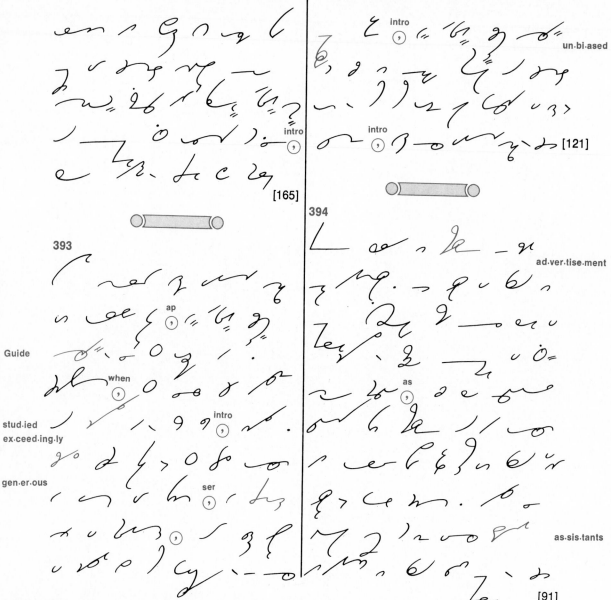

393

Guide

stud·ied
ex·ceed·ing·ly

gen·er·ous

394

ad·ver·tise·ment

as·sis·tants

[165]

[121]

[91]

Are you getting the full benefit from the spelling and punctuation helps in the Reading and Writing Practice by—

■ 1 Encircling all punctuation in your notes as you copy each Reading and Writing Practice?

■ 2 Noting the reason for the use of each punctuation mark to be sure that you understand why it was used?

■ 3 Spelling aloud at least once the words given in the margin of the shorthand?

RECALL

There are no new shorthand devices for you to learn in Lesson 42. However, this lesson does contain an Accuracy Practice and a review of the word beginnings and endings you have studied thus far. The Reading and Writing Practice contains some suggestions that you should heed carefully if you wish to get ahead in business.

Accuracy Practice

395   **My**   **Lie**   **Fight**

To write these combinations accurately:

■ a *Join the circle in the same way that you would join an* **a** *circle, but turn the* **end** *inside the circle.*

■ b *Before turning the* **end** *of the circle inside, be sure that the stroke touches the stroke to which the* **i** *is joined.*

■ c *Avoid making a point at the places indicated by arrows.*

practice drill

My, night, sight, line, mile.

396   Ow   Oi

To write these combinations accurately:

- **a** *Keep the hooks deep and narrow.*
- **b** *Place the circle* outside *the hooks as indicated by the dotted lines.*

practice drill

Out, now, doubt, scout, toy, soil, annoy.

397   Th   Nt, Nd   Mt, Md

To write these combinations accurately:

- **a** *Slant the strokes as indicated by the dotted lines.*
- **b** *Start these strokes to the right and upward.*

practice drill

There are, and will, empty, health, lined, ashamed.

Compare:

Hint, heard; tamed, detailed.

398 Recall Chart

This chart reviews word beginnings and word endings that you have studied. It has 90 words containing word beginnings and word endings. Can you read the entire chart in 4 minutes or less?

[Shorthand exercises in table, rows 1–15]

Building Transcription Skills

399
Business Vocabulary Builder

tribulations Trying experiences.

comprehend Understand.

similarities Likenesses.

significantly Considerably.

● Reading and Writing Practice

Reading Scoreboard The last time you measured your reading speed was in Lesson 30. See how much your reading speed has grown since Lesson 30. The following table will help you measure your reading speed on the *first reading* of Lesson 42.

Lesson 42 contains 454 words

If you read Lesson 42 in 12 minutes your reading rate is 38 words a minute
If you read Lesson 42 in 14 minutes your reading rate is 32 words a minute
If you read Lesson 42 in 16 minutes your reading rate is 28 words a minute
If you read Lesson 42 in 18 minutes your reading rate is 25 words a minute
If you read Lesson 42 in 21 minutes your reading rate is 22 words a minute
If you read Lesson 42 in 23 minutes your reading rate is 20 words a minute

---

If you can read Lesson 42 through the first time in less than 16 minutes, you are doing well.

400 Evaluate Yourself

[193]

(shorthand outlines)

un·fa·mil·iar

as

intro

com·pre·hend

achieve

par

of·ten

ap

tech·ni·cal

When you

when

ap

if

piece

sim·i·lar·i·ties

if

sig·nif·i·cant·ly

[261]

The Secretary Interacts With Others

No one in the business world needs greater skill in both human and public relations than the secretary. From the beginning to the end of the working day, the secretary must deal with people—instructing, asking, requesting, persuading, explaining, reminding, listening, cooperating.

Only when the principles of good human relations are observed in an office, can members of the business team work together successfully. Working well with others involves much more than merely getting along with people. It involves a conscious effort to exercise good judgment and tact, to feel concern for the problems and reactions of others, to show consideration for them and for their viewpoints, and to develop the personal character traits of loyalty, trust, and fairness.

Many situations arise every day in which the secretary will need the cooperation of co-workers. There will be other instances when the secretary will be asked to lend a hand to workers in other departments. These situations may involve working with other secretaries, receptionists, mailroom clerks, messengers, or copy-machine attendants. In addition, good working relationships must be developed with people outside the office. For example, the secretary might deal with a temporary personnel agency, a duplicating service, a machine-maintenance service, or even a florist.

It is necessary to maintain good human relations with all office personnel, but those with the employer are of paramount importance to the secretary. The successful secretary must have an excellent working relationship with the employer. This relationship must be based on mutual respect and understanding of the rights and responsibilities of each person.

Another of the secretary's important functions in human interactions is to maintain good relations with other company executives and, of course, with their secretaries. A secretary can contribute substantially to the employer's success by maintaining good human relationships between company offices.

Although the terms *human relations* and *public relations* are often used interchangeably, they do not mean the same thing. Human relations is based on understanding and responding to an individual or a group. Public relations is the technique of developing and keeping the goodwill of the public and the people with whom the company deals for the company and its employees.

The secretary's role as a public relations representative for the company is vital. It is the secretary to whom most customers and visitors first speak, either in person or by telephone. It is the secretary's voice or typed correspondence that says, "We are pleased to work with you."

Whether the situation involves dealing with another employee, a customer, a supplier, or a visitor, the secretary's skill in dealing with people is very important. The secretary's manner with co-workers, executives, or outside contacts has much to do with the overall success of the business.

Many secretaries consider the opportunities to meet and help others—whether from outside or within the firm—the most important job they do.

Principles

402 Word Beginning Mis-

The word beginning *mis-* is represented by *m-s*.

Spell: mis-t-a-k, mistake

mistake	misapprehension	misunderstanding
mistaken	misplaced	misunderstood
misprint	mislead	mystery

403 Word Beginning Super-

The word beginning *super-* is represented by a disjoined right *s*.

Spell: super-v-ī-s, supervise

supervise	superintendent	superior
supervisor	supervision	superb
supersede	superhuman	superimpose

404 U Represented by OO

The *oo* hook may be used after *n* and *m* to represent the sound of *u*, as in *music*.

Spell: m-oo-s-e-k, music

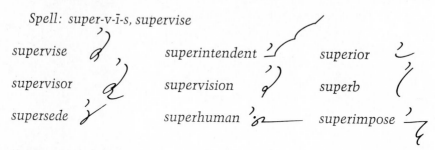

music	musical	communication
mutual	communicate	continue

Building Transcription Skills

405
PUNCTUATION
PRACTICE
, conjunction

A comma is used to separate two independent clauses that are joined by one of these conjunctions: *and, but, or, for, nor.*

An independent clause (sometimes called a main or a principal clause) is one that has a subject and a predicate and that could stand alone as a complete sentence.

There are 15 people in my department, but *only 11 of them are here now.*

The first independent clause is:

There are 15 people in my department.

And the second independent clause is:

Only 11 of them are here now.

Both clauses could stand as separate sentences, with a period after each. Because the thoughts of the two clauses are closely related, however, the clauses were joined to form one sentence. Because the two independent clauses are connected by the conjunction *but,* a comma is used between them and is placed before the conjunction.

Each time this use of the comma occurs in the Reading and Writing Practice, it will be indicated thus in the shorthand: _⌄

406
Business
Vocabulary
Builder

misapprehension Misunderstanding.

strikingly Impressively.

suitability Fitness.

● Reading and Writing Practice

407 **Brief-Form Review Letter**

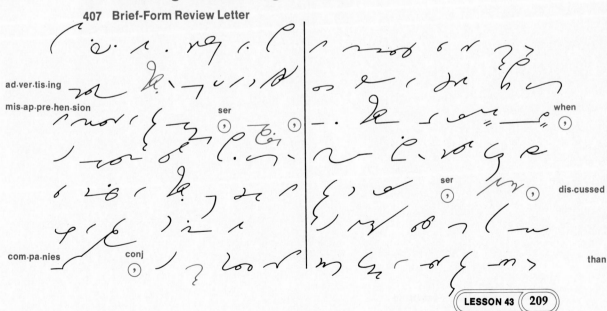

ad·ver·tis·ing

mis·ap·pre·hen·sion

ser

when

ser

dis·cussed

com·pa·nies

conj

than

bud·get
par
[150]

408

su·per·vi·sors
su·perb
ap
ser
han·dling

conj
so·lu·tions
conj
cou·pon
[194]

409

manu·script
conj
su·pe·ri·or
intro
ac·cept

if

re·view·er's

[139]

par

prompt·ly

[137]

410

Mys·tery

conj

intro

as

sci·en·tif·ic

yours

ar·ea

conj

411

as

re·spon·si·ble

ap

conj

ac·knowl·edg·ment

intro

quite

any·one

if

[98]

Principles

412 Word Beginning Self-

The word beginning *self-* is represented by a disjoined left *s*.

Spell: self-m-a-d, self-made

self-made	self-addressed	selfish
self-confidence	self-improvement	selfishness
self-reliance	self-assurance	unselfish

413 Word Beginning Circum-

The word beginning *circum-* is also represented by a disjoined left *s*.

Spell: circum-s-ten-s, circumstance

circumstance	circumstances	circumstantial

414 Word Ending -ification

The word ending *-ification* is represented by a disjoined *f*.

Spell: k-l-a-s-ification, classification

classification	notification	ratification
specification	gratification	modifications
justification	identification	qualifications

Building Transcription Skills

415
PUNCTUATION
PRACTICE
, and omitted

When two or more adjectives modify the same noun, they are separated by commas.

A stamped, addressed envelope is enclosed.

However, the comma is not used if the first adjective modifies the combined idea of the second adjective plus the noun.

The book was bound in an attractive brown *cloth.*

▶ Note: You can quickly determine whether to insert a comma between two consecutive adjectives by mentally placing *and* between them. If the sentence makes good sense with *and* inserted between the adjectives, then the comma is used. For example, the first illustration would make good sense if it read:

A stamped and *addressed* envelope is enclosed.

Each time this use of the comma occurs in the Reading and Writing Practice, it will be indicated thus in the shorthand: _{and o}

416
Business
Vocabulary
Builder

merger The combining of two or more business organizations.

upright Honest; conscientious.

trying *(adjective)* Difficult.

tedious Boring.

● Reading and Writing Practice

417 Brief-Form Review Letter

prob·a·bly

gov·ern·ment

as

par

conj

and o

cour·te·ous

priv·i·leges
con·ve·niences

ser

if

[161]

418

stud·ied

when

an·noyed

su·per·in·ten·dent

ap

[111]

419

up·right
cit·i·zens

and o

ser

prin·ci·ples

par

and o

en·ve·lope

[117]

420

para·graph

par

intro

valu·able [shorthand outline]

[shorthand outlines]

intro [shorthand outlines]

[shorthand outlines]

[shorthand outlines]

[shorthand outlines]

poise ser [shorthand outlines]

[shorthand outlines]

when [shorthand outlines]

con·vinc·ing·ly [shorthand outlines]

[shorthand outlines]

par [shorthand outlines]

en·roll·ing [shorthand outlines]

if [shorthand outlines]

156–1171 [shorthand] [166]

421

[shorthand outlines]

[shorthand outlines]

[shorthand outlines]

[shorthand outlines]

[shorthand outlines]

[shorthand outlines]

for·mal·ly [shorthand outlines]

as [shorthand outlines]

ap [shorthand outlines] ap·pre·ci·ate

and o conj te·dious [shorthand outlines]

[shorthand outlines]

com·mit·tee [shorthand] [124]

422

[shorthand outlines]

[shorthand outlines]

ap [shorthand outlines] 15 [shorthand]

[shorthand outlines] [33]

Principles

423 Word Ending -hood

The word ending *-hood* is represented by a disjoined *d*.

Spell: n-a-b-r-hood, neighborhood

neighborhood	boyhood	parenthood
childhood	girlhood	likelihood

424 Word Ending -ward

The word ending *-ward* is also represented by a disjoined *d*.

Spell: o-n-ward, onward

onward	awkward	forward
afterward	rewarding	forwarded
upward	backward	downward

425 UI

Ul is represented by *oo* when it precedes a forward or upward stroke.

Spell: re-s-ul-t, result

result	adult	multiply
consult	ultimately	culminate
consulted	culture	insulted

426 **Quantities and Amounts**

Here are a few more helpful abbreviations for quantities and amounts.

500	5	*$5,000,000,000*		*several hundred*	
$500		*a dollar*		*5 pounds*	
$5,000,000		*a million*		*8 feet*	

▶ Notice that the *n* for *hundred* is written *under* the figure as a positive distinction from *million,* in which the *m* is written *beside* the figure.

Building Transcription Skills

427
SPELLING
FAMILIES
-tion, -sion, -shion
An effective device to improve your ability to spell is to study words in related groups, or spelling families, that contain a common problem; for example, words ending in the sound *shun*. This sound is sometimes spelled *tion*, sometimes *sion*, and occasionally *shion*.

Practice each spelling family in this way:

■ 1 Spell each word aloud, pausing slightly after each syllable.

■ 2 Write each word once in longhand, spelling it aloud as you read it.

You will find many *shun* words in the Reading and Writing Practice.

Words Ending in -tion

ed·u·ca·tion	no·ti·fi·ca·tion	pub·li·ca·tion
in·for·ma·tion	cir·cu·la·tion	po·si·tion
or·ga·ni·za·tion	op·er·a·tions	re·la·tions

Words Ending in -sion

oc·ca·sion	pro·fes·sion	ex·ten·sion
di·vi·sion	dis·cus·sion	pro·vi·sion
ses·sion	de·ci·sion	re·vi·sion

Words Ending in -shion

fash·ion	cush·ion

428
Business
Vocabulary
Builder
ultimate Maximum; final.

prone Having a tendency or inclination.

insecure Uncertain.

● Reading and Writing Practice

429 Brief-Form Review Letter

430

ses·sion

com·put·er·iz·ing

ar·ea

prof·it·able
or·ga·ni·za·tion

neigh·bor·hood

ad·van·tage

ap

15

conj

and o

par

if

[181]

phys·i·cal·ly

prone

when

conj

ser

in·se·cure

awk·ward
and o

intro

ex·er·cise

stead

intro

bod·ies

[157] —Physical Fitness Council

431

and o

par

as

5
7

3
7

ser

mis·cel·la·neous

due

conj

re·mit·tance

intro

and o

en·ve·lope
prompt·ly
intro

[183]

432

and o

intro

① ②

LESSON 45 219

rise

ex·ceed·ing·ly   intro

spe·cial

if

[158]

433

col·ors

conj   pro·fes·sion·al

intro

intro   oc·ca·sion

[113]

BRIEF-FORM CHECKLIST *Are you making good use of the brief-form chart that appears on page 320? Remember, the brief forms represent many of the commonest words in the language; and the better you know them, the more rapid progress you will make in developing your shorthand speed.*

Are you—

- 1 Spending a few minutes reading from the chart each day?

- 2 Timing yourself and trying to cut a few seconds off your reading time with each reading?

- 3 Reading the brief forms in a different order each time—from left to right, from right to left, from top to bottom, from bottom to top?

Principles

434 Word Ending -gram

The word ending *-gram* is represented by a disjoined *gay*.

> *Spell:* t-e-l-gram, telegram

telegram _____   cablegram _____   programs _____

diagram _____   program _____   programmed _____

435 Word Beginning Electric-

The word beginning *electric-* (and the word *electric*) is represented by a disjoined *el*.

> *Spell:* electric-l, electrical

electric _____   electrically _____   electric wire _____

electrical _____   electric typewriter _____   electric motor _____

436 Word Beginning Electr-

The word beginning *electr-* is also represented by a disjoined *el*.

> *Spell:* electro-n-e-k, electronic

electronic _____   electricity _____   electrician _____

437 Compounds

Most compound words are formed simply by joining the outlines for the words that make up the compound. In some words, however, it is desirable to modify the outline for one of the words in order to obtain an easier joining.

anyhow	*ਟ਼*	someone	*ユ₂*	within	*ઉ*
anywhere	*e*	worthwhile	*ण○*	withstand	*ઉ*
thereupon	*ㄥ*	however*	*⁊*	notwithstanding	*⁊*

▶ *The dot may be omitted in *however*.

438 Intersection

Intersection, or the writing of one shorthand character through another, is sometimes useful for special phrases. This principle may be used when constant repetition of certain combinations of words in your dictation makes it clearly worthwhile to form special outlines for them.

| a.m. | *θ* | vice versa | *⁊* |
| p.m. | *ᵗ* | Chamber of Commerce | *⁊* |

Building Transcription Skills

439
SIMILAR-WORDS
DRILL
prominent,
permanent

prominent Notable; standing out.

ፖ ᒧ 2 . ᄂᵥ ⁊⁊

He took lessons from a prominent *musician.*

permanent Not subject to change; lasting.

ᵉ 2 . ᄂᵥ ⁊ ᵟ ⁊⁊

He was offered a permanent *job with the company.*

440
Business
Vocabulary
Builder

consultant One who gives professional advice or services; expert.

primarily Chiefly.

priority Something meriting first attention.

● Reading and Writing Practice

441 Brief-Form Review Letter

[Shorthand outlines with marginal word cues: con·sul·tant, ap, plane, for·tu·nate·ly, intro, par, Mu·nic·i·pal, ap, prom·i·nent, if]

[Right column shorthand with marginal cues: par, par, fee, [174]]

442

[Shorthand outlines with marginal word cues: when, some·one, per·ma·nent, elec·tri·cal, ser]

neigh·bor·hood

con·ve·nient

[141]

443

Su·pe·ri·or

shelves

man·u·als

pri·mar·i·ly

pro·fes·sion·al

en·joy·able

sou·ve·nir

[176]

444

intro

pro·gram·ming

em·ploy·ees

[106]

Principles

445 Geographical Expressions and Names

In geographical expressions and names, *-burg* is expressed by *b*; *-ingham*, by a disjoined *m*; *-ington*, by a disjoined *ten* blend; *-ville*, by *v*.

-burg

Spell: h-a-r-e-s-berg, Harrisburg

Harrisburg	Pittsburgh	Newburgh

-ingham

Spell: b-oo-k-ingham, Buckingham

Buckingham	Cunningham	Framingham

-ington

Spell: l-e-x-ington, Lexington

Lexington	Wilmington	Washington

-ville

Spell: n-a-ish-ville, Nashville

Nashville	Jacksonville	Evansville

Building Transcription Skills

446 GRAMMAR CHECKUP

Most executives have a good command of the English language. Some rarely make an error in grammar. There are times, though, when even the best dictators will perhaps use a plural verb with a singular noun or use the objective case when they should have used the nominative. They usually know better. In concentrating intently on expressing a thought or idea, however, they occasionally make a grammatical error.

It will be your job as a stenographer to catch these occasional errors and correct them when you transcribe.

From time to time in the lessons ahead you will be given an opportunity to brush up on some of the rules of grammar that are frequently violated.

GRAMMAR CHECKUP

comparisons

The comparative degree of an adjective or adverb is used when reference is made to two objects; the superlative degree is used when reference is made to more than two objects.

comparative

Of the two girls, Jane is the taller.

Which boy is more *efficient, Jim or Harry?*

Is Mr. Smith or Ms. Green better *qualified to do the job?*

superlative

Of the three boys, John is the tallest.

Which of the girls is the most *efficient, Jane, Mary, or Arlene?*

Is Mr. Smith, Ms. Green, or Mrs. Brown the best *qualified to do the job?*

447

Business Vocabulary Builder

fallacy A false idea.

unsurpassed The best; second to none.

extraordinary Remarkable; unusual.

● Reading and Writing Practice

448 **Brief-Form Review Letter**

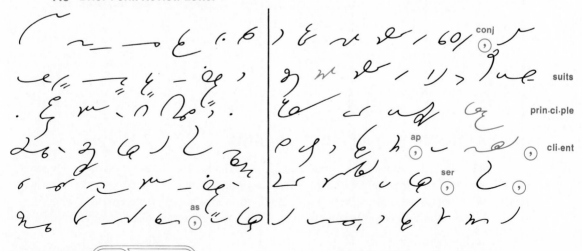

conj

suits

prin·ci·ple

ap

cli·ent

ser

as

cour·te·ous

and o

pleas·ant

neigh·bor·hood

when

un·sur·passed

and o

par

[187]

449

par

nat·u·ral·ly

intro

intro

ex·ten·sion

30

par

debts

[138]

450

par

enough

trans·ferred

intro

pass·book

par

[118]

451

ex·traor·di·nary

intro

sim·ple

and o

li·brary

[78]

452

intro

al·ready

intro

ef·fect

ser

and o

en·ve·lopes

par

[167]

RECALL

In Lesson 47 you studied the last of the new shorthand devices of Gregg Shorthand. In this lesson you will find an Accuracy Practice, a Recall Chart that reviews all the word-building principles of Gregg Shorthand, and a Reading and Writing Practice that contains some "food for thought."

Accuracy Practice

453   **Def**

To write this stroke accurately:

■ **a** *Make it large, almost the full height of your notebook line.*

■ **b** *Make it narrow.*

■ **c** *Start and finish the strokes on the same level of writing, as indicated by the dotted line.*

practice drill

Divide, definite, defeat, devote, differ, endeavor.

454   **Th**   **Ten**   **Tem**

To write these strokes accurately:

■ **a** *Slant the strokes as indicated by the dotted lines.*

■ **b** *Make the beginning of the curves deep.*

■ **c** *Make the* **tem** *large, about the full height of the line; the* **th** *small; the* **ten** *about half the size of the* **tem**

practice drill

In the, in time, tender, teeth, detain, medium.

455 Recall Chart

This chart contains illustrations of alphabetic characters, word-building principles, and phrasing principles of Gregg Shorthand.

WORDS

PHRASES AND AMOUNTS

16					
17					

Building Transcription Skills

456
Business Vocabulary Builder

accomplishments Achievements.

phase Aspect; side; part.

extensive Considerable.

● Reading and Writing Practice

457 Reading

lev·el

if

conj

Reading for Pleasure.

wheth·er

ser

dai·ly

intro

Intro

and o

worth·while

cit·i·zen

conj

well

Reading in School.

es·sen·tial

phase

col·lege

if

30

Reading on the Job.

ser

mis·cel·la·neous

intro

as

sur·vey

ap

par

ad·di·tion

intro

equip·ment

of·fered

when

sig·nif·i·cant·ly

[488]

Reinforcement

The Secretary's Day

There are as many secretarial job descriptions as there are employer-employee teams, and each job varies considerably from day to day. Although taking dictation and typing are an important part of the day's work, the secretary does many other things as well.

To give you an idea of what a typical day in the life of a secretary is like, imagine that you are secretary to Mrs. Ellen Garcia, marketing manager for a large textile company.

9:00 Arrive at the office. Check Mrs. Garcia's appointment calendar to make sure it agrees with yours. You notice that she has an 11 o'clock staff meeting, a luncheon appointment at 12:30 with Mr. Washington at the Cedar Inn, and a 3 o'clock appointment with Miss Rosen to go over the special department store promotion. A few minutes later, Mrs. Garcia arrives and you remind her of the meetings and appointments for the day. She gives you a corrected draft of a report to type for the staff meeting.

9:15 The morning mail is delivered. You open and sort it and bring it to Mrs. Garcia along with previous correspondence related to the incoming mail. Then you start typing the report.

9:30 Mrs. Garcia calls you in to take dictation.

9:45 You return to your desk to finish typing the report. The telephone rings several times and you provide information to those callers who don't need to speak to Mrs. Garcia personally. Mrs. Garcia asks for some information that must be obtained from the files. The company library calls and asks if Mrs. Garcia is finished with the book she borrowed. Someone else needs it. You check with Mrs. Garcia, and since she no longer needs the book, you take it back to the library.

10:30 You bring the completed report to Mrs. Garcia. While she is reading it, you check to make sure the conference room is ready for the meeting. Mrs. Garcia returns the report with no changes, so you make copies and distribute them for the meeting.

11:00 You make sure that all the materials are ready for the meeting. Then you begin transcribing. And the interruptions begin:

- You answer several telephone calls and take messages.

- Mrs. Garcia calls to ask you to bring a copy of this year's marketing plan to her in the conference room.

- You greet one caller who has come without an appointment. After checking the calendar, you set up a tentative appointment for 10 o'clock tomorrow.

11:45 The meeting is over and Mrs. Garcia stops at your desk to ask you to arrange a two-day trip to the Chicago office Monday and Tuesday of next week. You tell her about the appointment for tomorrow and when she agrees, you call the person and confirm.

12:00 You remind Mrs. Garcia of her luncheon date and then go to lunch yourself, after letting the receptionist know that you are leaving.

1:00 Return from lunch. You make all the necessary arrangements for Mrs. Garcia's trip, including transportation to and from the airports, plane and hotel reservations, and a rental car in Chicago. You type the itinerary and then you return to transcribing.

1:45 Mrs. Garcia returns with Mr. Washington and asks you to give him some papers he needs before he leaves. You get the papers and show him out.

2:00 Mrs. Garcia calls you in so she can start dictating a lengthy report. There are several interruptions; people stop to ask questions and the telephone rings.

2:50 The receptionist calls to say that Miss Rosen has arrived. You go to the reception area and escort her to the office.

3:00 You finish transcribing the morning's dictation.

3:15 Mrs. Garcia buzzes and asks you to bring in the samples of the new line.

3:30 Mrs. Garcia asks you to show Miss Rosen out and then bring your book so that she can continue dictating the report.

4:30 Mrs. Garcia decides to continue the report tomorrow. You prepare the correspondence for her signature. After she has signed the letters, you get them ready for the mail.

5:00 You clear your desk and tell Mrs. Garcia that you are leaving. You go home, knowing that you have worked hard today and that you will work just as hard tomorrow—but that tomorrow's schedule will be entirely different.

The letters in this lesson concentrate on the shorthand principles you studied in Chapter 1. You should have no difficulty reading them.

458 BRIEF FORMS AND DERIVATIVES

1. I, Mr., have, having, are-hour-our, ours-hours, will-well, willing, a-an, am, at-it, but.
2. In-not, increase, invite, indeed, is-his, that, can, cannot, you-your, yours, Mrs., of, with.

● Reading and Writing Practice

459

[57]

460

461

462

463

464

[73]

[58]

[59]

[47]

95.

80.

28.

29.

[64]

[53]

466

[64]

467

[41]

The practice material in this lesson concentrates on the shorthand principles you studied in Chapter 2.

468 BRIEF FORMS AND DERIVATIVES

1. *Be-by, before, began, believe, because, for, would, there (their), theirs, this.*
2. *Good, goods, they, which, them, and, when, from.*
3. *Could, send, sending, after, afternoon, street, streets, were, should.*

Building Transcription Skills

469
**Business
Vocabulary
Builder**

inspired Motivated.

fatal Causing death.

role Part.

● Reading and Writing Practice

470

[75]

471

15: 4

[81]

473

[95]

474

[87]

475

[94]

[109]

Lesson 51 concentrates on the shorthand principles you studied in Chapter 3.

476 BRIEF FORMS AND DERIVATIVES

1. *Gladly, worked, yesterday, circular, ordered, sooner, thank, enclosed, was.*
2. *Valuable, one (won), once, than, what, about, thing-think, thinks, businesses, doctor, anything.*
3. *Gentlemen, morning, important-importance, where, company, manufacturer, next, shortly.*

Building Transcription Skills

477

Business Vocabulary Builder

suitable Adapted to a use or purpose.

launching Originating or setting in motion.

● **Reading and Writing Practice**

478

[98]

479

[100]

480

[97]

481

[114]

482

[126]

LESSON 52

In this lesson you will receive a concentrated review of the shorthand principles you studied in Chapter 4.

483 BRIEF FORMS AND DERIVATIVES

1. *Presently, presents, part, parted, partly, advertise, advertisement, Ms., immediately, opportunities.*
2. *Advantage, advantages, suggestions, several, out, outside, ever-every, whenever, very.*
3. *Time, timed, acknowledgment, acknowledged, generally, questions, organization, overdue, overtime.*

Building Transcription Skills

484 SPELLING FAMILIES silent e dropped before -ing	Words in Which Silent E Is Dropped Before -ing		
	ad·ver·tis·ing	en·clos·ing	in·creas·ing
	de·sir·ing	ex·am·in·ing	pro·duc·ing
	de·cid·ing	forc·ing	pur·chas·ing
	dic·tat·ing	guid·ing	re·ceiv·ing

485
Business Vocabulary Builder

occur Happen.

appropriate *(adjective)* Especially suitable or fitting.

competent Able.

● Reading and Writing Practice

486

dic·ta·ting

wheth·er

sim·ply

de·cid·ing

ac·knowl·edge

[158]

487

per·son·nel

ad·ver·tis·ing

30

[117]

488

me·di·um

pur·chas·ing

po·ten·tial

[128]

489

healthy

sur·geon

[121]

490

years

con·fi·dent
de·rived

re·new·al

491

grat·i·fy·ing [55]

492

[100]

an·nounce

back·ground

re·or·ga·nize

[96]

SPELLING AND PUNCTUATION CHECKLIST

Are you careful to punctuate and spell correctly when—

■ 1 You write your compositions in English?

■ 2 Prepare your reports for your social studies classes?

■ 3 Correspond with friends to whom you must write in longhand?

In short, are you making correct spelling and punctuation a habit in all the longhand writing or typing that you do?

LESSON 53

In Lesson 53 you will practice many words and phrases that are written according to the principles you studied in Chapter 5.

493 BRIEF FORMS AND DERIVATIVES

(shorthand outlines)

1. *Difficulty, envelope, progressed, success, satisfy-satisfactory, state, statement, requested, underneath, wishing.*
2. *Particularly, probably, regularly, speaks, ideas, subject, regarded, newspaper, newspapers, opinions.*
3. *Responsible, worthy, publicly, publications, ordinary, ordinarily, experience, experienced, usually, world, recognized.*

Building Transcription Skills

494 **pressman** The operator of a printing press.

Business Vocabulary Builder

petition A formal written request.

depot A building for railroad or bus passengers or freight; a station.

● Reading and Writing Practice

495

(shorthand outlines)

rec·og·nized

prob·a·bly

ap·pre·ci·ate

en·ve·lope

[116]

Coun·cil

[113]

496

ar·ea

de·pot

shop·ping

497

le·gal

whose

phases

li·brary

[156]

498

phys·i·cal·ly

[94]

499

de·vot·ed

prac·ti·cal

[120]

LESSON 54

In this lesson you will have an opportunity to brush up on shorthand principles you studied in Chapter 6.

500 BRIEF FORMS AND DERIVATIVES

1. *Never, quantity, quantities, executive, throughout, object, objective.*
2. *Character, characters, governor, government, corresponded.*

Building Transcription Skills

501
SIMILAR-WORDS
DRILL
vacation, vocation

vacation A holiday; a period devoted to rest or relaxation.

I will take a short vacation in June.

vocation A regular occupation or profession.

My vocation is teaching.

502
Business
Vocabulary
Builder

creative Imaginative.

novel Original; new.

sites Places; locations.

● Reading and Writing Practice

503

Phoe·nix

vo·ca·tion

wheth·er

de·scribed

knowl·edge
cre·ative

par

ap

ser

par

ref·er·ence [144]

504

cop·ies

ap

de·spite

par

par

re·ceive [94]

505

par

nov·el

va·ca·tion

ser

sites

ap

ser

[132]

506

par

par

equal

par

no one

than

[138]

507

508

mod·ern

ad

sched·ule

par

par

ap

ap

par

380/

fur·ther

[108]

[103]

SHORTHAND NOTEBOOK CHECKLIST

Your shorthand notebook is another important tool of your trade. Do you:

■ **1** Use a notebook with a spiral binding so that the pages always lie flat as you write?

■ **2** Write on the front cover your name and the first and last dates on which you use the notebook?

■ **3** Place a rubber band around the used portion of your notebook so that it opens automatically to the first blank page?

■ **4** Date the first page of each day's dictation at the bottom of the page for quick and convenient reference—just as a stenographer in an office would do?

■ **5** Check before class to see that there are sufficient pages remaining in your notebook for the day's dictation and, if not, supply yourself with a second notebook so that you will not run out of paper in the middle of dictation?

LESSON 55

In Lesson 55 you will review shorthand principles you studied in Chapter 7.

509 BRIEF-FORM DERIVATIVES

[shorthand outlines]

1. *Suggested, corresponded, timed, organized, governed, manufactured.*
2. *Particularly, successfully, immediately, presently, gladly, partly, generally.*
3. *Sooner, manufacturer, speaker, sender, governor, timer, shorter.*

Building Transcription Skills

510
GRAMMAR
CHECKUP
the infinitive

The infinitive is the form of the verb usually introduced by *to—to see, to be, to have, to do.*

Careful writers try to avoid "splitting" an infinitive, that is, inserting a word or phrase between *to* and the following verb.

no

To properly do *the job, you need better tools.*

yes

To do *the job properly, you need better tools.*

no

He was told *to carefully prepare the report.*

yes

He was told *to prepare the report carefully.*

511
Business
Vocabulary
Builder

durability Ability to withstand wear; sturdiness.

inherited Received property by will.

reality The quality of being actual or true.

● Reading and Writing Practice

512

trans·fer·ring

be·com·ing

ap·ti·tude

re·ceive

phase

sal·a·ry

ex·ceed·ing·ly

[shorthand outlines]

if

ser

pho·to·graph

[154]

513

intro

intro

sta·tis·ti·cal

par

ser

de·pend·abil·i·ty

du·ra·bil·i·ty

pur·chase

[130]

514

in·her·i·ted

div·i·dend

trans·mit·ting

ti·tle

[123]

515

re·al·i·ty

- ser
- 18   19
- 20
- if
- grat·i·tude
- priv·i·lege
- ap
- 19   [158]

- intro
- clas·si·fied
- [137]

Left column (516):
- 516
- es·tate
- ser

Right column (517):
- 517
- an·nu·al
- ap
- dy·nam·ic
- 415–1177
- 10"   [63]

LESSON 56

The practice material in Lesson 56 will give you an opportunity to review shorthand principles you studied in Chapter 8.

518 BRIEF-FORM DERIVATIVES

1. *Government, apartment, departments, advertisement, acknowledgment, statement.*
2. *Circulars, encloses, executives, publications, wishes, progresses, objects, worlds.*
3. *Mornings, thanks, thinks, willingly, correspondingly, represent, reorganize.*

Building Transcription Skills

**519
COMMON
PREFIXES
super-**

In the English language there are many common prefixes. An understanding of the meanings of these prefixes will often give you a clue to the meaning of words with which you may be unfamiliar.

For example, you may never have encountered the word *superfluous*. However, if you knew that *super* meant *more than,* you probably could figure out that *super-fluous* means *more than enough.*

In each "Common Prefixes" exercise you will be given a common prefix, its meaning, and a list of words in which the prefix is used.

Read each definition and study the illustrations that follow. Several *super* words are used in the Reading and Writing Practice of this lesson.

super- over, more than

superior Over in rank; higher.

supervise To oversee.

supervisor One who oversees.

superfluous More than enough.

chore A routine task or job.

clarification The act of making clear or understandable.

● Reading and Writing Practice

521

te·dious

chore

kitch·en

[shorthand outline] [124]

522

lo·cal

con·fi·dent

neigh·bor·hood

when

con·ve·nient

[178]

523

manu·script

worth·while **and o**

rec·om·men·da·tion **intro**

par

conj

[146]

524

ap

col·li·sion

ap

intro

intro 2 **su·ing**

[107]

Shorthand & Transcription Skill Building

The Secretary Advances

Your first job is important because it will give you an opportunity to use the skills you have developed and to gain experience in making them work for you. Your ability to handle more important responsibilities will be gauged by the way you handle the duties assigned to you. In order to move up, you must first earn a reputation for reliability.

Promotion in secretarial work consists of moving up to jobs that are successively more important. A secretary may begin to work for a junior executive, advance to be secretary to a department head, then become secretary to a corporate officer, and finally, advance to a position of secretary to the president of a company or chairman of the board of directors.

From the outset it is important to establish a good record. Remember, you are your own best friend when it comes to progressing on the job. By doing your best work on every assignment, by sharpening and improving your skills, and by welcoming new responsibilities as chances to prove your abilities, you will open doors for promotion for yourself.

In order to generate new opportunities for yourself, you must keep adding to your inventory of professional abilities. Continue to learn, and you will increase your value to your employer. Improve your work procedures and accuracy, and take advantage of opportunities for extra service.

Keep up with changes in the business world. Participate in professional activities outside the job by taking additional training and joining a professional secretarial association. These and similar activities will enhance your value in the office and in the company.

If you want to move ahead, you have to think ahead. Achieving excellence and earning promotions rarely occur by chance; they are likely to occur when you look ahead, choose your goals, and then work hard to achieve them.

LESSON 57

Lesson 57 is a "brief form" lesson. It contains one or more illustrations of *every* brief form in Gregg Shorthand. Counting repetitions, there are 452 brief forms or derivatives. Because you have seen and written all of these brief forms many, many times, you should be able to complete this lesson in record time!

Building Transcription Skills

525
SPELLING
FAMILIES
-able, -ible

A difficult spelling problem for stenographers is deciding whether a word ends in *-able* or *-ible*. Unfortunately, there is no rule that tells us when to use *-able* and when to use *-ible*. In a majority of English words the ending is spelled *-able*, but it is spelled *-ible* in a sufficient number of words that you should think twice before you type an *a* or an *i*. In the following list dots are placed in the words where they may be divided on the typewriter.

Words Ending in -able

avail·able	prob·a·ble	re·li·able
com·fort·able	prof·it·able	suit·able
de·sir·able	rea·son·able	valu·able

Words Ending in -ible

de·duct·ible	im·pos·si·ble	re·spon·si·ble
flex·i·ble	pos·si·ble	sen·si·ble

526
Business
Vocabulary
Builder

defray To provide for the payment of.
administer Supervise; manage.
forcefulness Effectiveness.

● Reading and Writing Practice

527

[shorthand outlines]

chil·dren

fam·i·ly

if

suc·cess·ful

and o

re·spon·si·ble

and o

suit·able

re·quest

when

intro

par

[177]

528

Op·por·tu·ni·ties

ap

busi·nesses

siz·able

ser

intro

com·pa·ny's

par

im·me·di·ate·ly

par

prof·it·able

en·ve·lope

[158]

529

gov·ern·ment

ap·pli·ca·tion

intro

han·dling

conj

intro

yours

par

sat·is·fy·ing [147]

530

ap

Tues·day

[79]

531

Shorthand outline with annotations: ser, im·pres·sive, 1850, twelfth, 12, if [125]

532

Shorthand outline

Shorthand outline with annotations: ser, dis·sat·is·fied ser, if, and o [89]

533

Shorthand outline with annotations: 18, 20 [64]

534
Transcription Quiz
In Lessons 31-56 you have studied nine rules for the correct use of the comma. In Lessons 57-69 you will have an opportunity to test your mastery of these rules through a "Transcription Quiz"—a letter in which no commas are indicated in the shorthand.

It will be your job, as you copy the letter in shorthand in your notebook, to insert the commas in the proper places and to give the reasons why the commas are used.

The shorthand in your notebook should resemble the following example:

As you probably know, (, as) I will be in Dallas on Friday, (, ap) August 4.

At the head of each Transcription Quiz you will find the number and types of commas the letter calls for.

The correct punctuation of the following letter calls for 5 commas—1 comma *as* clause, 1 comma conjunction, 2 commas series, 1 comma *if* clause.

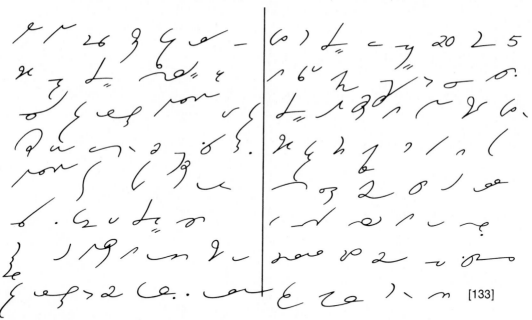

[133]

PERSONAL-USE CHECKLIST *Do you substitute shorthand for longhand wherever possible when you—*

- 1 Take down your daily assignments?
- 2 Correspond with your friends who know shorthand?
- 3 Draft compositions and reports?
- 4 Make notes to yourself on things to do, people to see, appointments to keep, etc?

This lesson provides you with an opportunity to increase your phrasing skill. It contains many illustrations of the phrasing principles of Gregg Shorthand. All told, it contains 102 phrases, counting repetitions.

Building Transcription Skills

535
GRAMMAR
CHECKUP
sentence
structure

Parallel ideas should be expressed in parallel form.

no

I hope our relationship will be long, pleasant, *and* of profit *to both of us.*

yes

I hope our relationship will be long, pleasant, *and* profitable *to both of us.*

no

As soon as we receive the necessary information, your account will be opened *and* we will ship your order.

yes

As soon as we receive the necessary information, your account will be opened *and* your order will be shipped.

It is especially important to keep parallel all ideas in a tabulation.

no

The secretary's main duties were:
    1. Taking dictation and transcribing
    2. Answering the telephone
    3. To take care of the files

yes

The secretary's main duties were:
    1. Taking dictation and transcribing
    2. Answering the telephone
    3. Taking care of the files

536
Business
Vocabulary
Builder

complications Difficulties.

county A territorial division for local government within a state.

geared Adjusted in order to satisfy something.

● **Reading and Writing Practice**

537

[shorthand outlines]

Christ·mas

par (,)

par (,)

as (,)

owe
pur·chased

en·ve·lope   and o (,)

[127]

538

when (,)

115–1118

conj (,)   cour·te·ous

shipped

40,

if (,)

per·son·al

540
Transcription Quiz

The correct punctuation of the following letter calls for 5 commas—1 comma *when* clause, 2 commas parenthetical, 2 commas series.

[102]

Lesson 59 provides an opportunity for you to brush up on the joined word beginnings of Gregg Shorthand. In the letters of this lesson there are 80 words containing joined word beginnings.

Building Transcription Skills

541
SPELLING
FAMILIES
-cial, -tial

Be very careful when you transcribe words ending in the sound of *shul*. The ending is sometimes spelled *-cial*, sometimes *-tial*.

Words Ending in -cial

ben·e·fi·cial	fi·nan·cial	so·cial
com·mer·cial	of·fi·cial	spe·cial

Words Ending in -tial

es·sen·tial	ini·tial	po·ten·tial
in·flu·en·tial	par·tial	sub·stan·tial

542
Business
Vocabulary
Builder

conversion Something changed from one use to another.

colleagues Associates; co-workers.

convalesce To recover health gradually after sickness.

● Reading and Writing Practice

543

un·for·tu·nate·ly

conj

de·spite

em·ploy·ees intro

sub·stan·tial and o

en·cour·ag·ing

com·mer·cial if

con·ver·sion when

apol·o·gize

[153]

544 ap

li·brary

thor·ough·ly conj

de·light·ed par

[100]

545

spe·cial ap

ini·tial intro

ex·haust·ed

per·son·al par

conj

ad·ver·tis·ing

ser

if

[98]

546

conj

1166

conj

ap

[112]

547 The correct punctuation of the following letter calls for 6 commas—2 commas con-
Transcription Quiz junction, 2 commas parenthetical, 1 comma *as* clause, 1 comma introductory.

[108]

Lesson 60 concentrates on joined word endings. There are 88 words containing them in this lesson.

Building Transcription Skills

548
COMMON
PREFIXES
re-

re- again

replenish To fill or supply again.

repeat To say or do again.

reconsider To take up again.

reconfirm To assure again.

renew To make like new again.

549
Business
Vocabulary
Builder

mark down *(verb)* Reduce the price of.

portable Capable of being carried or moved about.

humid Moist.

● Reading and Writing Practice

Reading
Scoreboard

Here is your chance to determine how much your reading speed has increased over your first score in Lesson 18.

Lesson 60 contains 767 words

If you read Lesson 60 in **17 minutes** your reading rate is **46 words a minute**

If you read Lesson 60 in **19 minutes** your reading rate is **40 words a minute**

If you read Lesson 60 in **22 minutes** your reading rate is **35 words a minute**

If you read Lesson 60 in **25 minutes** your reading rate is **31 words a minute**
If you read Lesson 60 in **27 minutes** your reading rate is **28 words a minute**
If you read Lesson 60 in **30 minutes** your reading rate is **26 words a minute**

550

[shorthand outlines]

rep·u·ta·ble

debt

cred·i·tors

leath·er

re·plen·ish

ward·robe

[157]

551

rep·e·ti·tion

hu·mid

de·pend·able

won't

[140]

552

and o

intro

sig·na·ture .

24 ⌇ ⌇ ⌇ 7 − 48
⌇ ⌇ ⌇ . 36 =

ser

and o · if

worth·while

[113]

553

par

par

en·vi·able

intro

intro

ser

ef·fi·cient·ly

when

[127]

554

un·sealed

con·fi·den·tial
grate·ful

par

ne·ces·si·tates

intro

[104]

555 As you copy the following letter in your notebook, be sure to indicate the necessary
Transcription Quiz commas at the proper points and to indicate the reason for the punctuation.

The letter calls for 5 commas—2 commas series, 1 comma apposition, and 2 commas parenthetical.

[126]

The disjoined word beginnings of Gregg Shorthand are treated extensively in Lesson 61. In the Reading and Writing Practice of this lesson, you will find 47 words containing disjoined word beginnings.

Building Transcription Skills

556
GRAMMAR
CHECKUP
subject and verb

A verb must agree with its subject in number.

Our representative is *taking care of your needs.*

Your bills *for April* are *enclosed.*

The inclusion of a phrase such as *in addition to, as well as,* or *along with* does not affect the number of the verb. If the subject is singular, use a singular verb; if the subject is plural, use a plural verb.

Our representative, *as well as our managers,* is *looking forward to the pleasure of serving you.*

Your *canceled* checks, *along with your statement,* are *mailed to you each month.*

557
Business Vocabulary Builder

effects *(noun)* Physical property; goods.

buffet A counter for refreshments.

frustrating Disappointing.

● Reading and Writing Practice

558

re·cent·ly   su·per·vi·so·ry   ap

[shorthand outlines]

ed·i·to·ri·al

if

ap

[134]

559

adopt·ed

ap

, 15 ,

de·sir·able

when

ser

ef·fects

as

em·ploy·ee

ah

[114]

560

buf·fet

lc 14

lc 14

lc 14·

par

bro·chure

oc·ca·sion
cit·ies

[138]

561

man·u·al

intro

as
1940
ap
intro

de·scribes

par

[134]

562 In the letter that follows you must supply 4 commas to punctuate it correctly—1
Transcription Quiz comma conjunction, 1 comma introductory, 1 comma *and* omitted, 1 comma
if clause.

[148]

LESSON 62

Here is an opportunity for you to improve your grasp of disjoined word endings in Gregg Shorthand. In this lesson there are 47 words containing disjoined word endings.

Building Transcription Skills

563
SIMILAR-WORDS
DRILL
their, there, they're

their Belonging to them.

Some people make their *own clothes.*

there In or to that place.

The students went there *at my request.*

they're Contraction for *they are.*

They're *always ready to serve you.*

564
Business
Vocabulary
Builder

discomfort Annoyance.

purification The act of cleaning.

impartial Fair; showing no favoritism.

● Reading and Writing Practice

565

[shorthand outlines]

their
neigh·bor·hood

[shorthand outlines]

ap ,

[shorthand outlines]

jus·ti·fied

conj ,

and o ,

rec·om·men·da·tions

[shorthand outlines]

intro ,

par , ,

pro·ceed

conj ,

they're

par ,

when ,

[157]

566

[shorthand outlines]

conj ,

veg·e·ta·ble

[shorthand outlines]

conj ,

whole

[shorthand outlines]

as ,

chem·i·cals

pu·ri·fi·ca·tion

if ,

en·gi·neers

[shorthand outlines]

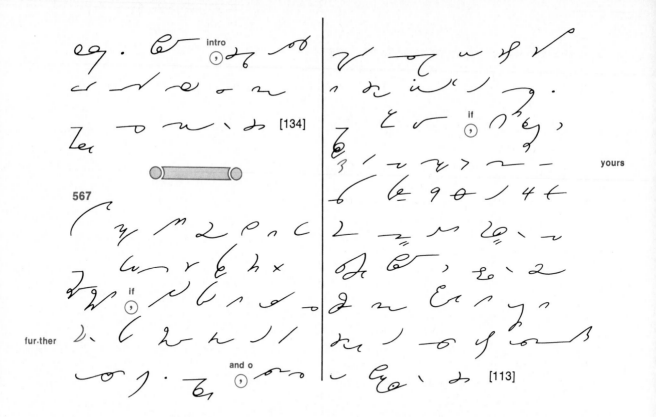

intro

[134]

567

further

if

and o

yours

[113]

568
Transcription Quiz The following letter requires 6 commas—2 commas parenthetical, 2 commas series, 1 comma apposition, 1 comma introductory. Can you supply these commas?

[107]

In dictation your employer will frequently use numbers. Because of the great importance of accuracy in transcribing numbers, you should take special care to write numbers legibly in your notes. The material in this lesson will help you fix more firmly in your mind the various devices for expressing numbers and quantities in Gregg Shorthand.

Building Transcription Skills

569
COMMON
PREFIXES
un-

un- not

    unusual Not ordinary; rare.

    uncertain Not sure.

    unprecedented Not having been done before.

    unnecessary Not needed.

    unquestioned Not disputed.

570
Business
Vocabulary
Builder

processed *(verb)* Moved along.

pledged Guaranteed; promised.

depressed *(adjective)* Suffering from low economic activity.

● Reading and Writing Practice

571 Tons of Food

[shorthand outlines] 70   14

weight

loaves

ser

3

her·ring

ser

veg·e·ta·bles

ser

ser

ad·di·tion   intro

ser

cheese

[144]

—Your Health

572

ap

pro·cessed

as

conj   pur·chased

plea·sure

par

and o   pleas·ant

[136]

573

un·ques·tioned

pledged

15 ... (20,)

intro

or 10 / ... 12 / [144]

when

un·prec·e·dent·ed
achieve·ment

par

[144]

574
Transcription Quiz The following letter requires 6 commas—1 comma *if* clause, 4 commas parenthetical, 1 comma *when* clause. Remember to indicate these commas in your shorthand notes and to give the reason for their use.

① "120—

② "90—

③ "55—

④ "2—

[125]

As you learned during the early stages of your study of Gregg Shorthand, vowels may be omitted in some words to help you gain fluency of writing. In this lesson you will find many words illustrating the omission of vowels.

Building Transcription Skills

575
SPELLING
FAMILIES
-er, -or, -ar

Words Ending in -er

bak·er	cus·tom·er	re·mind·er
con·sid·er	of·fi·cer	speak·er

Words Ending in -or

col·or	gov·er·nor	op·er·a·tor
doc·tor	ma·jor	pro·fes·sor

Words Ending in -ar

dol·lar	pop·u·lar	schol·ar
gram·mar	reg·u·lar	sug·ar

576
Business
Vocabulary
Builder

enviable Highly desirable.

dynamic Forceful.

constructive Promoting improvement or development.

● Reading and Writing Practice

577

[shorthand outlines] wheth·er

Marginal word cues (left column): ide·al, ad·di·tion, ser, intro, par, cour·te·ous, and o, if, ap, intro, and o

Marginal word cues (right column): en·vi·able, of·fer·ing, ser, stretch, intro, gen·u·ine, ap, aware, conj, par, com·pli·ments, when, as, guest

Shorthand annotations: if, ser, ap, intro, par, and o, [133]

Paragraph numbers: 578, 579

for·tu·nate
ap
par
ap
dy·nam·ic

for·ward

[144]

580 For you to supply: 5 commas—1 comma *if* clause, 1 comma introductory, 2 commas
Transcription Quiz series, 1 comma *when* clause.

[131]

LESSON 65

One of the reasons why Gregg Shorthand can be written so fluently and rapidly is its blends—single strokes that represent two or more sounds. In the Reading and Writing Practice of this lesson you will find 113 words containing blends.

Building Transcription Skills

581
SIMILAR-WORDS
DRILL
brought, bought

brought The past tense and past participle of *bring*.

They brought the books back after they had read them.

bought Purchased.

Thousands of companies have bought our Model 116 computer.

582
Business Vocabulary Builder

intense Considerable.

refineries Plants for purifying oil.

commendation Praise.

● Reading and Writing Practice

583

en·er·gy

ex·am·ple

intro

de·vel·op·ment

ser

as

mer·chants

com·men·da·tion

bought

ap

intro

brought

lo·cal

conj

when

if

conj

ex·cel·lent

par

vi·tal
ur·gent·ly

and o

[136]

584

585

[118]

res·i·dence 〔shorthand outline〕 hours

par

au·to·mat·i·cal·ly 〔shorthand outline〕 intro

enough

de·spite

ser

ap intro

114

par intro

/ 151–1161 〔outline〕 [109] brought

intro bought

586

if

114

114

intro [173]

587

Man·age·ment

ap

wit

intro

[130]

588
Transcription Quiz For you to supply: 7 commas—2 commas apposition, 4 commas series, 1 comma *if* clause.

[120]

LESSON 66

This is another lesson that concentrates on brief forms. Counting repetitions, it contains 267 brief forms and derivatives.

Building Transcription Skills

589
COMMON
PREFIXES
pro-

pro- in many words *pro-* means *before, ahead, forward,* or *future.*

proceed To go ahead.

progress A forward movement.

prospect A possible future customer.

promotion The act of moving ahead.

procedure A manner of going ahead.

590
Business
Vocabulary
Builder

anticipation The act of looking forward.

in arrears Behind in payment; overdue debt.

● Reading and Writing Practice

591

its

intro ⟨,⟩

conj ⟨,⟩

im·me·di·ate·ly

intro

any·one

when

ar·rears

intro   and o

log·i·cal

en·ve·lope

pro·ceed

trans·fer·ring

if

[134]

[146]

593

as

prob·a·bly

592

ap·pli·cants

ac·knowl·edge

conj

qual·i·ties

ser

ap

pro·ceed

par

conj

re·mit·tance

conj

duties

worth·while

conj
（,）

and o
（,）

chal·leng·ing

ar ‿ [178]

594
Transcription Quiz   For you to supply: 5 commas—3 commas introductory, 1 comma conjunction, 1 comma *if* clause.

[141]

LESSON 67

Here is another opportunity for you to increase your skill in writing phrases. In this lesson there are 114 phrases.

Building Transcription Skills

595
GRAMMAR
CHECKUP
verbs with
"one of"

In most cases, the expression *one of* takes a singular verb, which agrees with the subject *one*.

One of *the people on the staff* is *ill*.

One of *our typewriters* does *not work*.

When *one of* is part of an expression such as *one of those who* or *one of the things that*, a plural verb is used to agree with its antecedent in number.

Kay solved one of the problems that have (*not* has) *been annoying us for years*.

Lee is one of the students who drive (*not* drives) *to school*.

596
Business
Vocabulary
Builder

bearable Capable of being borne.

eventful Momentous; full of events.

milestones Significant points in development.

● Reading and Writing Practice

597

bi·cy·cle

par

re·lieved

as

con·va·les·cence
bear·able

[87]

598

ap·pre·ci·ate

ap

15.

conj

re·ceive

when

else·where

par

par

im·pressed

than

[130]

599

ap

an·ni·ver·sa·ry

15.

16

par

conj

mile·stones

ser

suc·cess·ful

conj

intro

won't [shorthand] [134]

600 [shorthand with annotation: as] [shorthand]

[shorthand] [104]

[annotations: par, and o, pros·per·ous]

601
Transcription Quiz For you to supply: 6 commas—1 comma conjunction, 1 comma *as* clause, 1 comma apposition, 1 comma *and* omitted, 2 commas parenthetical.

[shorthand] [129]

Lesson 68 contains a general review of many of the major principles of Gregg Shorthand.

Building Transcription Skills

602
SIMILAR-WORDS DRILL
some, sum

some A portion.

) 2 6 Re n x

Have some *of our services displeased you?*

sum Amount; total.

n u) r 2 u 5/ ~

You owe us the sum of $500.

603
Business Vocabulary Builder

incredibly Hardly believable.

judicious Having sound judgment; wise.

net income Earnings remaining after expenses.

frankness Honesty.

● Reading and Writing Practice

604

in·cred·i·bly

sum

ju·di·cious

en·gi·neers

ser

ser

if

[127]

605

its

intro

and o

eco·nom·i·cal
than

of·fer·ing

conj

if

ap

leaf·let

[142]

606

as

ap

[20]
[10]
[20]
[30]
[30]
[15]
[13]
24,

607

re·ceive

sum·ma·ry

when (,)

intro (,)

[130]

[87]

608 For you to supply: 4 commas—3 commas parenthetical, 1 comma *if* clause.

Transcription Quiz

[101]

LESSON 69

You probably won't be able to refrain from chuckling as you read the "hotel" letters in the Reading and Writing Practice. They are an exchange of letters by the manager and a guest with a sense of humor.

Building Transcription Skills

609
COMMON
PREFIXES
pre-

pre- before; beforehand.

    predict To tell beforehand; to prophesy.

    preliminary Coming before the main business.

    premature Happening before the proper time.

    presume To assume to be true before proof is established.

610
Business
Vocabulary
Builder

desolated Sad; unhappy; disappointed.

conceivably Possibly.

establishment Place of business.

● Reading and Writing Practice

611

cus·tom·ary
guest's

oc·cu·pied

intro

of·ten

par

ser

intro

intro

par

[95]

612

des·o·lat·ed

ap

sou·ve·nirs

vis·i·tor

zoo
con·ceiv·ably

par

par

run·ning

as

thought·ful·ly

draw·er

intro

maid

when

es·tab·lish·ment

[258]

613
Transcription Quiz
For you to supply: 5 commas—1 comma *and* omitted, 1 comma introductory, 1 comma conjunction, 2 commas parenthetical.

[141]

VOCABULARY
CHECKLIST

Has your command of words improved since you began your study of Gregg Shorthand? It has if you—

- 1 Studied all the words in the Business Vocabulary Builders and added them to your everyday vocabulary.

- 2 Paid careful attention to the Similar-Words Drills, so that you know the difference between *addition, edition; some, sum,* etc.

- 3 Learned the meanings of the common prefixes presented in a number of the lessons of your textbook.

LESSON 70

When you are employed in a business office, you will have occasion to use the telephone frequently. The information in the Reading and Writing Practice will help you use the telephone efficiently.

Building Transcription Skills

614
SPELLING
FAMILIES
-ize, -ise, -yze

Be careful when you must type a word ending with the sound of *iz*. The ending may be spelled *-ize, ise, or -yze.*

Words Ending in -ize

apol·o·gize	re·al·ize	uti·lize
or·ga·nize	rec·og·nize	vi·su·al·ize

Words Ending in -ise

ad·ver·tise	com·prise	rise
ad·vise	en·ter·prise	su·per·vise

Words Ending in -yze

an·a·lyze	par·a·lyze

615
Business
Vocabulary
Builder

moderate *(adjective)* Reasonable.

offensive *(adjective)* Giving unpleasant sensations.

visualize To form a mental image of; to see.

commending Praising.

● Reading and Writing Practice

Reading
Scoreboard

Now that you are on the last lesson, you are no doubt very much interested in your final shorthand reading rate. If you have followed the practice suggestions you received early in the course, your shorthand reading rate at this time should be a source of pride to you.

To get a picture of how much your shorthand reading rate has increased with practice, compare it with the reading rate in Lesson 18, the first time you measured it.

Lesson 70 contains 778 words

If you read Lesson 70 in 15 minutes your reading rate is 50 words a minute
If you read Lesson 70 in 19 minutes your reading rate is 41 words a minute
If you read Lesson 70 in 22 minutes your reading rate is 35 words a minute
If you read Lesson 70 in 26 minutes your reading rate is 30 words a minute
If you read Lesson 70 in 29 minutes your reading rate is 27 words a minute
If you read Lesson 70 in 32 minutes your reading rate is 24 words a minute

616 The Telephone

Volume.

of·fen·sive

em·pha·sis

A Pleasant Voice.

par

and o

Telephone Courtesy.

agree·able

re·al·ize

ex·ten·sion

intro

if

than

vi·su·al·ize

ser

in·ter·rupt

rec·og·nize

if

Receiving Calls. ︙

when

track

when

when

Transferring Calls.

qual·i·fied

if

dis·turb·ing

as

al·ready

ir·ri·tat·ing

fur·ther

intro

[680]

617 Appreciation

praise

par

when

[98]

Appendix

States

The abbreviations in parentheses are those recommended by the Postal Service.

Alabama [AL]

Alaska [AK]

Arizona [AZ]

Arkansas [AR]

California [CA]

Colorado [CO]

Connecticut [CT]

Delaware [DE]

Florida [FL]

Georgia [GA]

Hawaii [HI]

Idaho [ID]

Illinois [IL]

Indiana [IN]

Iowa [IA]

Kansas [KS]

Kentucky [KY]

Louisiana [LA]

Maine [ME]

Maryland [MD]

Massachusetts [MA]

Michigan [MI]

Minnesota [MN]

Mississippi [MS]

Missouri [MO]

Montana [MT]

Nebraska [NE]

Nevada [NV]

New Hampshire [NH]

New Jersey [NJ]

New Mexico [NM]

New York [NY]

North Carolina [NC]

North Dakota [ND]

Ohio [OH]

Oklahoma [OK]

Oregon [OR]

Pennsylvania [PA]

Rhode Island [RI]

South Carolina [SC]

South Dakota [SD]

Tennessee [TN]

Texas [TX]

Utah [UT]

Vermont [VT]

Virginia [VA]

Washington [WA]

West Virginia [WV]

Wisconsin [WI]

Wyoming [WY]

Selected Cities of the United States

Akron	Dayton	Louisville
Albany	Denver	Memphis
Anchorage	Des Moines	Miami
Atlanta	Detroit	Milwaukee
Baltimore	El Paso	Minneapolis
Baton Rouge	Fairbanks	Montpelier
Birmingham	Fargo	Nashville
Boston	Fort Worth	Newark
Bridgeport	Grand Rapids	New Orleans
Buffalo	Hartford	New York
Cambridge	Honolulu	Norfolk
Camden	Houston	Oakland
Charleston	Indianapolis	Oklahoma City
Charlotte	Jacksonville	Omaha
Chattanooga	Jersey City	Philadelphia
Cheyenne	Kansas City	Phoenix
Chicago	Knoxville	Pittsburgh
Cincinnati	Laramie	Portland
Cleveland	Las Vegas	Providence
Columbia	Lincoln	Richmond
Columbus	Little Rock	Rochester
Dallas	Los Angeles	Sacramento

St. Louis		Shreveport		Toledo	
St. Paul		Spokane		Trenton	
Salt Lake City		Springfield		Tucson	
San Antonio		Syracuse		Tulsa	
San Diego		Tacoma		Washington	
San Francisco		Tallahassee		Wichita	
Seattle		Tampa		Wilmington	

Common Geographical Abbreviations

America		England		Canada	
American		English		Canadian	
United States		Great Britain		Puerto Rico	

The Metric System

If you take dictation in which there are many occurrences of metric measurements, you will have frequent use for the abbreviated forms given below. It is not wise to attempt to learn these forms until you know you will have use for them.

The metric system was devised by France and adopted there by law in 1799. Since that time its use has become almost universal except in Great Britain and the United States. It is rapidly coming into use in those two countries and, therefore, it is possible that you will need these special outlines. If the terms occur only infrequently in your dictation, it is better to write them in full.

The following abbreviations will be useful to those who must frequently take metric measurements in dictation.

		meter	liter	gram
kilo-	1,000			
hekto-	100			
deka-	10			

		meter	liter	gram
deci-	1/10			
centi-	1/100			
milli-	1/1,000			
micro-	1/1,000,000			
nano-	1/1,000,000,000			

ADDITIONAL METRIC MEASUREMENTS

Celsius		*kilowatt*		*microsecond*	
centigrade		*kilowatt-hour*		*milliampere*	
cubic centimeter		*megabit*		*millibar*	
kilobit		*megahertz*		*millifarad*	
kilocalorie		*megaton*		*millihenry*	
kilocycle		*megawatt*		*millimicrosecond*	
kilohertz		*megohm*		*millivolt*	
kiloton		*micromicron*		*milliwatt*	
kilovolt		*micron*		*nanosecond*	

Index of Gregg Shorthand

In order to facilitate finding, this Index has been divided into six main sections—Alphabetic Characters, Brief Forms, General, Phrasing, Word Beginnings, Word Endings.

The first figure refers to the lesson; the second refers to the paragraph.

INDEX OF BRIEF FORMS

The first figure refers to the lesson; the second to the paragraph.

INDEX OF BUILDING TRANSCRIPTION SKILLS

The first figure refers to the lesson; the second figure to the paragraph.

Brief Forms of Gregg Shorthand

IN ORDER OF PRESENTATION

A	B	C	D	E	F	G